Picture Poems

Volume 3

Thomas G. Reischel

Word Art Publishing
9350 Wilshire Blvd
Suite 203, Beverly Hills, CA 90212
www.wordartpublishing.com
Phone: 1 (888) 614 - 1370

Published by Word Art Publishing

ISBN: 978-1-955070-72-0 (Hardcover)
ISBN: 978-1-955070-62-1 (Paperback)
ISBN: 978-1-955070-63-8 (eBook)

DEDICATION

· ·

To my wife Karen, who always holds
my hand, and my sister Marilee
Ashwanden, who has always
encouraged me to publish my poetry.

INTRODUCTION

· ·

This is the third and final volume in this series of Picture Poems. This volume contains the last nine chapters of 50 poems. In this set, the largest category of poems is under the Scene category. I think you'll find this a very diverse and intriguing chapter. Some of my most favorite and unique poems are in there. But first, I'll begin with a discussion of my purpose, and a short poetry primer. If you read my previous volumes, you have already seen this before. If not, here it is.

I believe that photography and poetry go together well. One form paints a visual picture while the other creates a poetic image. Together, the synergy becomes very powerful. At least, that is what I hope I have achieved here. This book contains both. All the photographs contained in this book were taken by the author and the poetry was also written by him.

The author resides in St. Paul, Minnesota, USA. The photos were all taken within the state. So, besides the esthetic journey, he hopes the book also provides the reader a bit of information about the place that is his home.

Besides the poem itself, the author will typically add author's notes. These notes generally try to provide three bits of information. First will be a comment about the poem itself. Second, a description of the poetic format is provided. Finally, the author may comment about the photograph. This is provided to be informational. It may be redundant or unnecessary for some. Those individuals can skip over what they want, part or even all of the notes. They are there for those who appreciate them.

So, this book is really meant for several types of readers. There will be those who merely want to see the photographs. I think that is wonderful, and hope that my photography is sufficiently good enough to satisfy their craving. Others will just like the poetry. Again, although I don't purport to be an expert, I hope that I have at least accomplished some success and have whetted their appetite for more. Some may want to focus on style and format, and I believe this book should appeal to them as well.

In addition, I hope this book becomes a learning tool for some. I believe that it might appeal to both poetry teachers, as well as poetry students. To that end, I have added a lot of information about poetic techniques. This book contains examples of 35 different types, or formats, if you will. I have included a Glossary of Poetry Type that I used at the back of this book.

The chapters have been organized by the category of photograph for the picture lovers, then in alphabetical order of the poem's title. There are chapters with Animal/Wildlife, Birds, Insects, Flowers, Gardens, Pathways, Scenes, Sunrise and Sunsets, to please the eye.

The author doesn't claim to be an authority in these areas, so please allow him a bit of poetic license.

For those, who are new to poetry, I need to give a bit of information that may help you understand poetry better. This is necessary because I refer to these standard forms of poetic schematics frequently within my author's notes. So this section is intended to help a reader grasp the references adequately, but not be a detailed poetry education. This is fairly technical, but I'll try to explain it as simply as possible. I didn't invent this system; it has been around a long time. I am merely going to explain some of it to you here. Those who are already familiar can skip this part of the introduction, unless you feel you need a refresher.

Poetry comes in many styles and forms. My poems identify what the style it is meant to be. Let's start with a discussion of rhyme. Poems may or may not have rhyme. The rhyme is usually at the end of each line and is known as "end rhyme". If not at the end, it is known as "in-line rhyme". As you read my poetic descriptions, I may refer to the end rhymes in an alphanumeric code. For example, the first rhyming word in a poem is referred to as the "a" rhyme, and every line in the poem that rhymes with it is designated the letter "a". The second rhyme to occur would be identified as "b", the third as "c", and so on. The most common poem has 4 lines (a Quatrain). The most typical end rhyme schemes for a quatrain are:

aabb (Coupled Rhyme)
abab (Alternating Rhyme)
abba (Enveloping Ryme)
abcb (Skipping Rhyme)

Poems may contain a paragraph. These are known as stanzas. These Stanzas may contain the same rhyme or may vary. Here are examples of the rhyme scheme of a poem with two stanzas.

aabb baba (Here the rhyme was the same in both, but one was coupled while the other was alternating).

aabb ccdd (Here each stanza has two different coupled rhymes)

Poems may also contain one or more repeating rhyme. That means it has the same identical rhyme word. This is usually identified using a capital letter, like so

Abab Abab (Here I'm referring to the first line of each stanza)

It could also mean a complete repeating line or refrain. That would be identified in the author's notes.

Poems may also have varying numbers of lines. Here is a list of the most common:

Couplet: 2 Lines
Tercet: 3 Lines
Quatrain: 4 lines
Quintet or Quintrain: 5 Lines
Sestet: 6 Lines
Sextet: 7 lines
Octet or Octive: 8 lines

Poems can also mix stanza styles. For example, a Sonnet usually contains 3 quatrains and a couplet (14 total lines).

Poems also may contain a structured syllable count. This establishes the rhythm at which the poem is read. This is known as meter. Typically these are paired in sets of two, known as a foot. There is a name for each type of meter, as follows.

Two syllables - Monometer (one foot)
Four syllables - Dimeter (two Feet)
Six syllables - Trimeter (three feet)
Eight syllables - Tetrameter (four feet)
Ten syllables - Pentameter (five feet)
Twelve syllables – Hexameter or Alexandrian (six feet)
Fourteen syllables - Heptameter (seven feet)
Sixteen Syllables - Octameter (eight feet)

The ones most common or frequently used are Tetrameter and Pentameter.

The most complex poetic concept focuses around syllable accents, whether they are hard or soft, and how they are linked together. The most common of these are iambic and the trochaic (trochee) meters. As you speak a word, there is an accent on each syllable that results in either a soft or a hard sound. For example the word cowboy puts the hard accent on the first syllable – **COW**boy. The word police, puts the hard accent on the second syllable – po**LICE**. How you string words together determines the type of meter. Iambic meter alternates soft -hard, soft- hard. For example, Shakespeare's famous words –"To be or not to be" is iambic: to **BE** or **NOT** to **BE**. But the second half is not iambic – **THAT** is the **QUES**tion. Iambic is frequently defined as da-Dum, da-DUM type meter, where each da-Dum is a poetic foot. Therefore, iambic pentameter would carry a meter of: da-**DUM**, da-**DUM**, da-**Dum**, da-**DUM**, da-**DUM**. Trochee is exactly the opposite of iambic, where each line starts with a hard syllable accent and ends with a soft. **TWIN**kle **TWIN**kle **LIT**tle **STAR** how **I** won**DER** what **YOU** are.

In volume 2, I added some more detail than I had in volume 1. For each poem I listed in detail some of the poetic techniques employed, such as: alliteration, assonance, in-line rhyming. I hope readers will appreciate my pointing these things out as it is not my intention to bore them, but rather I hope it may bring additional depth of appreciation to the poetry. If not, feel free to skip over that part.

Here is a description of a few poetic techniques available.

Alliteration: The use of repetitive first letters (usually consonants) at the beginning of words. Often these words are consecutive, but don't necessarily need to be. Alliteration occurs when the same letters (or sound, such as ph and f) are repeated more than once in a line of poetry. In a structured poem, such as one with quatrains or couplets, the distinction of what constitutes a line is pretty clear. Below is an example of alliteration used in a couplet in poem 41, Cherub Fountain and poem 40, Casting shadows, where the poetic line is pretty clear.

(From Poem 41, Vol. 2)

Yon cherubs *dance delightfully* in sky. These little water nymphs *pleasantly play*

(From Poem 40, Vol. 2)

Watchers don't *want* the *scene* to end too *soon*.

It's amazing, when that *golden* orb *glows*.

It's a bit different in a Free Verse Poem, where the line is not as distinct. There, the alliteration occurs within a phrase or completed thought. Below is an example of alliteration within a Free Verse from Poem 49, The Pond, Vol. 2.

Then I turned a corner
and
beheld
a **wooden** *bench beside* the sparkling **water**.

Assonance: The repetition of similar vowel sounds within a line of poetry, but not at the beginning of the words. Below is an example of the assonance expressed by the U sound in a line from Poem 29, Silken Swirls, Vol. 2.

Rich the *hues* this *bush imbues*,

Consonance: The repetition of similar consonant sounds within a line of poetry, but not at the beginning of the words. This line from Poem 12, Baltimore Orioles, Vol. 2 provides an example of the consonance created by the TW sound.

Sitting *twixt the twigs*, raising spirits high,

In-line Rhyme: Where one or more rhymes occur within a line of poetry, rather than between end- lines. The rhyme may match the end-rhyme, or any other word in that line, or both. The following lines from Poem 15, The Coot's Call, Vol 2, is an example. The in-line rhyme is on the first line below. "Great" rhymes with the end-line rhyme "fate", which rhymes with "mate".

The chance is *great*; he'll find love's *fate*.
In tall swamp grass a Coot did hide,
So lonely, looking for a mate.

Onomatopoeia: This is the use of words that denote a sound or the feel of a sound. For example, "Oink" is the sound made by a pig. "Swish" isn't a sound, but gives the feel of a sound. An example comes from poem 43, Fido on the Roof, Vol. 2.

Looked across the street this morning,
There was a doggy on the roof.
The surprise came without warning
When I was startled by a *"woof"*.

Anaphora: The repeated use of a word or phrase at the beginning of a phrase, line, or stanza, that provides an impact or to underline a point in poetry, or speeches for that matter. The most famous use of Anaphora was "I have a dream", by Martin Luther King Jr. For an example of this technique, see Poem 14, Comes the Muse, Vol. 2.

Caesura: A pause or stop in a line of poetry, usually with some form of punctuation.

Now, in Volume 3, I added some more complex poetic techniques, and highlighted them in the notes of each Poem. The poet uses these to enhance the character of the poem. Some poems were so large that I couldn't get in everything, as I limited my poem, plus notes, to one page. So, to keep it shorter, I did not identify consonance or assonance in this volume. But most of the others I did, if they were present, and I had room. Here are some of the new concepts I added.

Colloquialism: is a variety of language commonly employed in conversation or other communication in informal situations. The word colloquial originally referred to speech as distinguished from writing, but is fundamentally about the degree of informality or casualness. It can include dialects, like when a pirate says "yer mangy seadog, "or "aye, matey." In any case, it usually sounds familiar. Here is an example from Poem 37, Broken Base, Vol. 3.

Assemble all the gears that turn.
Rebuild the broken base anew.
The time has come to live and learn.
Deliverance is overdue.

Connotation: using words that connote a suggestive meaning to it. There can be negative or positive connotations. Associations called up by words that go beyond their dictionary meaning. For example, when you call a person "yellow." In Poem 40, Free Will, the word "path" connotes a choice, while the word "plateau" can mean floor, or a phase of life.

The paths we take may lead us high or low.
If we're uncertain, there's a map to show
the choices that prevail at each plateau.

Ekphrastic: is a vivid description of a scene or, more commonly, a work of art. An Ekphrastic poem is a poem inspired or stimulated by a work of art or stunning photograph. Since all my poem are based on my photographs, they all are Ekphrastic. When I refer to that term in a poem, I am pointing out that it is unusually descriptive. Poem 7 is a good example, as the entire poem is very descriptive.

Elision: is when a word is shortened by dropping a letter or syllable out of it, in order to preserve the meter of a line. The missing element is replaced by an apostrophe. The word is still recognizable. See Poem 22, Bursting Bloom, Vol. 3.

to light the darkest ev'ning skies.
So too, this bloom seems to my eyes.

Exhortation: is a command to do something, like "go there," or 'listen!" I use that quite a bit in Poem 37, Broken Base, Vol. 3. Here's a snippet.

Assemble all the gears that turn.
Rebuild the broken base anew.
The time has come to live and learn.

Folksy Language: is language, similar to colloquialism that is friendly chatter. Poem 18, Landing Goose, Vol. 3, has an example.

Canada
May be in your name
You're kinda
Quite fonda
The grasses of Bermuda

Humor: is the quality of being amusing or comic, especially as expressed in literature or speech. That quality which appeals to a sense of the ludicrous or absurdly incongruous. A good example is Poem 2, Going Ape, Vol. 3, where I used it throughout. Here's a glimpse.

Excuse me if I bite my tongue.
Forgive the leaks my mind has sprung...
I'm going ape over you!

Hyperbole: is gross exaggeration. This verse from Poem 10, Colored Hue, Vol. 3, is a good example.

Colors of purple, bronze, and gold,
It must be told,
Upon the ground,
Delights abound!

Irony: is a contrast or discrepancy between what is said and what is meant, or between what happens and what is expected to happen. Here is an line from Poem 50, Sunshine Finally Pierces, Vol. 3.

Another day to savor, before I die.

Kinesthesia: is the sensation or perception of motion, as I did in Poem 17, Eagle, Vol. 3.

Elegantly swooping, first left, then right.

Personification: is giving inanimate objects, or abstract concepts, the qualities of living things (feelings, actions, characteristics). These lines form Poem 10, Colored Hue, Vol. 3, show it well.

Wrought iron gates or cobbled walk,
If they could talk,
They would but sing.

Question: is when the poet adds in a question to the poem. This helps to draw the reader in, so that they become involved. An example of that can be found in Poem 28, Purple Vetch, Vol. 3.

To my surprise, what did I see?
A Canada Anemone!

Simile: Often confused with Metaphor, Simile is using a comparison between two things very specifically, by introducing the comparison with the words "as," "like," or "as though." I did that in these lines from Poem 13, These Golden Trees, Vol. 3.

The branches form a color dome,
as lovely as an arch in Rome

Speaker Technique: Writing the Poem as if we imagine the person or thing to be the one speaking. The voice behind the poem. Here is an example from Poem 4, Little Bunny, Vol. 3.

You see I'm often shy, as I
Will run or hop away.

Today I'm here, without much fear,
On such a pleasant day.

Warning: is when the object of the poem, or a stanza, is to provide a warning about some described danger. Poem 21, Bittersweet Nightshade, Vol. 3, does that.

So clearly centered on bright yellow shoots,
May attract curious children to them.
Beware of tiny red poisonous fruits!

There are many more techniques. I don't purport to have listed them all here. These are just the ones that I used and identified in this set of Poems

Well, that's about as deep as I want to get.

I welcome you to join me with this next set of 50 poems. Hope you enjoy them as immensely as I enjoyed writing them.

ACKNOWLEDGEMENTS

. . . .

I'd like to recognize and thank my understanding wife, Karen Lynne (Sweetnam) Reischel, for providing support by reading all my poems as they were created and making helpful suggestions, as well as being the final editor. I'd also like to thank all my FanStory friends and fans who also helped and encouraged me. Finally, the staff at Word Art Publishing who provided their valuable assistance, especially Beau Brandon whose patience and persuasion over several years has gotten me here. Thank you all for your time and effort. For without it, this book could never have been possible.

TABLE OF CONTENTS

CHAPTER 1: ANIMALS/WILDLIFE

. . . .

To the poet, wildlife presents a wonderful palette on which to paint poetic pictures of their antics and the moods that they create in the viewer while being observed.

They are wonderful subjects to photograph, whether they are: deer, squirrels, buffalo, horses, fish, monkeys, or whatever. They may be in the wild or in a zoo; in a forest or a lake. No matter where they are found, they are always interesting.

Poem #1

BUFFALO
(Modified Rondel)

Roaring thunder across the plains,
Buffalo herds once ruled the age,
In numbers far too vast to gauge,
Muscle on hooves with mangy manes.

Legendary long passing lanes,
Took days to reach the final stage,
For pioneers in wagon-trains,
Buffalo herds once ruled the age,

Until they came on iron trains,
When bison hunters turned the page,
Roaring thunder across the plains,
Buffalo herds once ruled the age.

Carcasses rot, as rifles reign,
Millions gone, to the red man's rage.
Systematic genocide waged,
Roaring thunder across the plains.

Today in parks or small zoo cage,
Only echoes of past remains,
Roaring thunder across the plains,
Buffalo herds once ruled the age.

A great slaughter of the buffalo herds of North America occurred in the 1800's. In a systematic genocide of the Native Americans and because ranchers wanted to fence off their land, the herds were killed off. Estimated to be between 40 and 60 million, they were killed to near extinction by buffalo hunters who shot all day long leaving the bodies to rot, taking only the tongue and some hides. This was a main food source for the plains Indians. By the time they finished, only about 750 remained of the vast herds the pioneers said took days to pass their wagon trains as they headed west. The introduction of the iron horse (trains) facilitated movement and funding of the buffalo hunters.

This poem is a modified Rondel.

I took the general format of a Rondel for this poem and modified it to be similar to the Rondeau poem. The first and second lines repeat in the middle of the poem and at the end. The rhyme scheme is normally:

ABba abAB abbaA.

For this poem I inserted an additional stanza and rearranged the order a bit. My rhyme scheme is:

ABba abaB abAB abbA baAB, where the capitals represent the repeated lines.

The syllable count is 8.

Alliteration: muscle mangy manes, legendary long lanes, rifles reign, red rage.

Metaphor: Roaring thunder, Muscle on Hooves, turned the page, echoes of past.

This photograph was taken by the author at the Como Zoo in St. Paul, Minnesota on a November day, 2012. Inclusion of the chain link was intentional.

Poem #2

GOING APE

(Tercets)

Don't know how life is going to go,
But there is one thing that I know...
I'm going ape over you!

Sometimes confused, sometimes surprised,
There is something can't be disguised...
I'm going ape over you!

Excuse me if I bite my tongue.
Forgive the leaks my mind has sprung...
I'm going ape over you!

My voice is tangled up today.
There's only one thing I can say...
I'm going ape over you!

In visiting the zoo, I thought this monkey reminded me of Golem, from the Lord of the Rings movie. . It got me thinking romantically, nevertheless.

I had a day full of monkey shines at the zoo. This fellow is a Chimpanzee,

This poem is written with Tercets.

Tercets are three line poems. A Haiku is an example of an unrhymed Tercet poem. A poetic Triplet is a Tercet in which all three lines follow the same rhyme, (a a a) Triplets are rather rare. Other types of Tercets include an enclosed Tercet where the lines rhyme in an a b a pattern and Terza Rima where the a,b,a pattern of a verse is continued in the next verse by making the outer lines of the next stanza rhyme with the central line of the preceding stanza, b,c,b, as in the Terza Rima or Terzina form.

These are some interlinked Tercets, with a rhyme scheme of:

aaB ccB ddB eeB

The meter is:

8-8-7

The repeated line echoes throughout the poem, and adds the intended touch of humor.

I also used a few Colloquialisms.

This picture is from my photo collection. Another one from Como Zoo.

Poem #3

ENJOY THE KOI
(Mixed Meter Quatrains)

I enjoy all the Koi
That swim in shallow pools.
They bring a bit of sunshine
In the shadows, dark and cool.

They move about the pond
In groups of curiosity.
This one white, that one gold,
A black one then makes three.

I see so many in the pools.
Gather together in schools.
Colors flash as they flit around,
Leaving impressions most profound.

If you stick in tempting finger,
Thinking it's a worm to eat,
The whole school will linger.
Remove it, they'll retreat.

Such colorful torpedoes
That add to the watery hues,
Have flashes of orange and indigos
That will chase away any blues.

Koi are colorful relatives of the Gold Fish family that grow larger and come in several colors. Koi, literally "brocaded carp", are ornamental varieties of common carp that are kept for decorative purposes in outdoor Koi ponds or water gardens. Carp are cold water fish, and their ability to survive and adapt to many climates and water conditions allowed the domesticated species to be propagated. Carp were first bred for color mutations in China more than a thousand years ago, where selective breeding of the Prussian carp (Carassius gibelio) led to the development of the goldfish. The common carp was grown as a food fish at least as long ago as the fifth century BC in China, and in the Roman Empire during the spread of Christianity in Europe. Source Wikipedia.

This poem is Unmetered Quatrains.

Here, I threw out the restrictions of metered and numbered verse. I just went for it. So it becomes Mixed Meter. However, there is a rhyme scheme: abcb (Skipping), aabb (Coupled) and abab (Alternating). So I've used most of the conventional rhyme schemes, except Enveloping, in this poem. Can you tell which is which?

When I said that they move in groups of curiosity, I was using poetic Imagery.

Alliteration: Swim shallow, bring bit, this that, see so, flash flit, remove retreat.

In-line Rhyme: enjoy Koi

This photograph was taken by the author at the Japanese Garden at Como Park in St. Paul, Minnesota.

Poem #4

LITTLE BUNNY
(Rhyming Quatrains)

Oh, to be one little bunny!
What wonders would I see,
As I apprise with rabbit eyes,
The world surrounding me?

The world surrounding me is large,
And I'm a little soul.
Sometimes it's such a scary place,
I hide out in my hole.

I hide out in my hole on days
When raptors ride on high,
Coyotes stalk, or owls soar.
You see, I'm often shy!

You see I'm often shy, as I
Will run or hop away.
Today I'm here, without much fear,
On such a pleasant day.

On such a pleasant day, the sun
Shines brightly on the trail,
While I search out a tasty snack
I'll rest my cotton-tail.

I'll rest my cotton-tail, because
I saw you standing there
With camera ready to shoot
A picture of a Hare.

I was on a walk with my grandson at the Upper Landing area along the Mississippi in St. Paul, Minnesota, when along the path we spotted this little bunny. My grandson, Jeremy T. Hamlin, had my Kodak 981 digital camera, so he knelt down and took this photograph. It made our day, which was Thursday, August 22, 2013. He was a happy 9 year old photographer. He tried to get it to come over and sniff his hand, but after posing for us, it hopped off.

This poem is just some simple quatrains in an easy going abcb rhyme scheme and with an 8/6 syllable count.

I did use the poetic device of using the 6 count last line of the verse as the first line of the next stanza, by adding two more syllables, thus expanding it to 8 syllables.

In this poem I used the Speaker Technique (A.K.A.- Dramatic Monologue), and spoke in the First Person.

I used a Question Technique to draw the reader in.

Alliteration: what wonders would, as apprise, sometimes such scary, hide hole, raptors ride, stalk soar, see shy, search snack.

In-line Rhyme: apprise eyes

This picture is part of the author's personal collection.

Poem #5

MOMMA KILLDEER
(ABAB Quatrains)

I came upon a mother Killdeer
Pretending she was wounded.
With absolutely nothing to fear,
Her worries were unfounded

She was peeping like a maniac,
And fluttering all about,
With a ruckus like a cardiac
Victim's heart that's giving out.

I know that she was simply trying
To protect her little nest.
The problem that seems underlying
Was, her choice wasn't the best.

She chose to pick a nice location
By a tree among the rocks.
Her decision brought aggravation
Where a golfer often walks.

Since she put it in a busy place
Where traffic was sure to be.
It was inches from the parking space,
Of a golf course's first tee.

A Killdeer is a brown and white bird on tall thin legs that nests on the ground. It is distinguished by 3 black stripes across its chest and forehead. I discovered this particular one the other night while golfing. As I pulled my cart up to the first tee box, it started peeping loudly, in a very high-pitched, annoying screech. It flew around wildly, then landed nearby, and stuck out its wing. It was hopping about like it was wounded. That is its method to distract predators away from its nest by projecting the image of an easy meal.

This poem is ABAB Rhymed Quatrains.

The set of abab rhymed quatrains is written with a pulsating meter of 9-7-9-7. It is done in mixed meter.

The Cardiac verse of the second stanza uses Simile.

Caesura was used in Stanza 3, line 4, to create a dramatic pause.

Alliteration: was wounded, worries were, all about, since she, where was.

This photograph was taken by the author himself at Emerald Greens Golf Course in Hastings, Minnesota at the tenth hole tee box on June 17, 2014.

Poem #6

PERENGRINE FALCON
(ABCB Rhymed Quatrains)

A swift air rider
Seeker of the heights
Peregrine Falcon
Fleet of wing in flight

A lofty hunter
Other birds its prey
Whose burst of speed
Takes your breath away

It drops from the heavens
At lightning's pace
From above the victim
It decides to chase

With its life-long partner
Seeks a cliff or ledge
In a quiet corner
To let young ones fledge

As the fastest creature
On the planet Earth
It is trained at hunting
For its sporting worth

A swift air rider
Seeker of the heights
Peregrine Falcon
Fleet of wing in flight

If you spot one soaring
In the morning sky
Watch this wandering wonder
As it passes by

The Peregrine Falcon is an amazing bird. It is a member of the Raptor family, along with Eagles and Owls. It hunts in the air and attacks from above other birds, and even bats, by diving from on high at very high speed, using its sharp talons to capture its victims. It has been clocked at speeds between 200 and 250 MPH, making it the fastest member of the animal kingdom. The bird mates for life, making its nest in high places, such as mountain cliffs or even on ledges of skyscrapers. The name, Peregrine, means wanderer. They are known to travel far and wide, but often return to their favorite nesting area. Peregrines are found nearly everywhere, making them the most widespread bird species known. They are prized by Falconers for their trainability and hunting skill.

Fledge - to grow flight feathers.

This poem is a set of ABCB Rhymed Quatrains. The Quatrain is a poetic stanza consisting of four lines. I wrote this one with a variable meter of short lines ranging from 4 to 6 syllables. The rhyme scheme is the Skipping Rhyme of abcb, which is the simplest of all the rhyme schemes, because it only uses two rhymes for every four lines of the poem.

No punctuation was used. Many poems read fine without it. I felt here, that adding punctuation would take away its lightness.

I used metaphor in "at lightning's pace."

I used the technique of repeating an entire stanza to add flair and balanced.

Alliteration: fleet flight, life long, watch wandering wonder.

This picture was taken by the author in September of 2012 at Fort Snelling State Park in St. Paul, Minnesota during a presentation by the Raptor Center.

Poem #7

POND AND FROG
(Cinquains)

A pond,
of which I'm fond,
where I am often seen,
in film of algae covered slime
was green.

Where frog,
skin green and black,
with spots upon its back,
was a camouflaged exhibit.
Ribbet!

You can't hide from me, Mr. Frog!

OK, I was being a bit playful with this poem. You often hear frogs before you see them, although this one was hiding. Or so it thought.

This poem is two Cinquains.

A Cinquain is written using a pattern. "Cinq" [pronounced SINK] is French for the number 5. This type of poem only has five lines. Each line follows a specific pattern.

There are many ways to write this type of poetry. The traditional Cinquain, as developed by Adelaide Crapsey, has five lines and a strict structure based on syllable count.

Line 1: Two syllables Line 2: Four syllables

Line 3: Six syllables Line 4: Eight syllables

Line 5: Two syllables

It can be free versed or rhymed. I chose to rhyme it. The rhyme scheme is:

aabcb abbcc.

I used poetic imagery to describe where it was located in slime, and its color.

I used Onomatopoeia on the last line.

Since this poem also describes the picture completely, it is an Ekphrastic poem.

This frog picture is from the author's collection and is the reason this poem was written. It was taken in August 2012, at Maplewood Nature Center.

Poem #8

SWISH
(A Pleiades Poem)

Swish that sweet tail without fail
Swing on past the corral rail
Sway this way without delay
Sweep all distractions away
Swat trouble on the double
Swirl away fretful rubble
Swipe a wipe with that fine tail

The Tale of the Tail

Well, don't you just love being engaged with a horse's rear end? I spotted this group along a highway, and stopped to take a snapshot.

This poem is a Pleiades Poem.

According to Poetry Dances (a poetic Glossary on the FanStory site), this style of poem has a title with a single word. The poem itself has seven lines. The first word in each line begins with the same letter as the title. There is no requirement of rhyme or syllable count or meter. Not a very difficult style to achieve. I thought that this format was too simple and tame, so I added some challenge to it.

I have all the first two letters match.

Each starting word, in addition, is similar in meaning and related to an action that a tail makes.

I added a rhyme scheme. This one is:

aabbcca.

The syllable count on all seven lines is 7.

I threw in some inline rhyme and alliteration.

Alliteration: swish sweet, way without, wipe with.

In-line Rhyme: tail fail, sway way delay, trouble double, swipe wipe.

Onomatopoeia: Swish

This picture is from my personal photograph collection and is the reason I wrote this poem in the first place.

CHAPTER 2: AUTUMN/SPRING

· ·

Who doesn't find the burst of new life in the Spring, or the fantastic colors of Autumn, inspiring? Certainly they are both candidates for the photographer's eye and the poet's pen. I really enjoy getting out the camera bags and lenses to capture the images. Those images fascinate my muse and drive it to create flowing verse. Here in these pages, I have tried to capture the essence of both. I hope that you agree.

Poem #9

COLOR DOESN'T STOP
(A Free Style Poem)

When the leaves
have changed their colors
on the trees of
my home town,

the color doesn't stop
at every stop,

but continues on

forever,

for each
appreciating eye.

Before they drop,
You'll see

a canopy
of   color
in the sky.

To delight the visual senses,
of the harried
passersby,

and
excite the delight
of drivers
in their cars,

with all of
Autumn's
color
repertoires.

This is a street in downtown St. Paul, Minnesota, near the Cathedral area, in autumn color. With those cars and stop signs so apparent the inspiration was a natural.

This is a Free Style Poem

A Free Style poem is like Free Verse, except is has rhyming. A Free Style Poem is a subset of Free Verse. It has no rhyme scheme, tempo, or meter pattern. It just flows with the words. The author adds dimension in how the poem is felt, through the use of pace and pause, created in how the words are arranged on the page. The distinction between Free Style and Free Verse is that Free Style contains some rhyme while Free Verse does not. It rhymes in places as the author wants, but not necessarily consistently.

Alliteration: changed colors, each eye, canopy color, delight drivers.

Hyperbole: forever, harried passersby

Kinesthesia: changed colors, stop, continue on, they drop.

Metaphor: canopy of color, repertoires.

Poetic Imagery: leaves have changed their colors, appreciating eye, canopy of color, delight the visual senses, excite the delight, drivers in their cars, Autumn's colors.

Personification: color doesn't stop

This picture was taken by the author in October, 2012.

Poem #10

COLORED HUE
(A Minute Poem)

The Autumn leaves in colored hue,
All coming through
For you to view,
As people do.

Wrought iron gates or cobbled walk,
If they could talk,
They would but sing.
A wondrous thing!

Colors of purple, bronze, and gold,
It must be told,
Upon the ground,
Delights abound!

Autumn is coming. I can't wait to see the glorious color hues again. This group is just a sampling of the colors that abound. I see some purple, red, brown, yellow, and green in this one. Just a set of leaves, yet so much more. This was in a corner of a yard along Selby Avenue, in St. Paul. I shot this while my wife was in the Harvest Bakery picking up some fresh baked bread. I felt this poem should be jaunty and upbeat.

This poem is a Minute Poem.

The Minute Poem is a poem that follows the "8,4,4,4" syllable count structure. It usually has 3 stanzas that are exactly the same. So:

8,4,4,4; 8,4,4,4; 8,4,4,4 syllables.

A traditional Minute Poem has 12 lines total. It has 60 syllables (thus, the Minute). It is written in a strict iambic meter. This one is iambic tetrameter, but is can be any iambic.

The usual rhyme scheme is as follows: aabb, ccdd, eeff, but I made the first stanza in this poem Mono-syllable as well.

Hyperbole: A wondrous thing, It must be told, delights abound.

In-line Rhyme: you to view.

Personification: Cobbled walk could talk or sing.

Poetic Imagery: colored hue, wrought iron gates, cobbled walk, colors purple, bronze, and gold.

Onomatopoeia: talk, sing.

This picture was taken by the author last fall, October, 2012.

Poem #11

COLORFUL CORNER CANOPY
(A Zejel Poem)

Autumn's painted on every tree,
Nature's beautiful leaf marquee,
Colorful corner canopy.

Tree limbs arching over the street,
Arrayed in Autumn's finest treat.
This season's style show can't be beat.
Such a wonderful sight to see.

The colors blaze with orange and red.
Bronze and yellow are also shed,
That pile up on the walks we tread,
To jump and kick through joyously.

Still a touch of lingering green
Prevails upon Fall's color scene,
Combines to make it so serene.
With just a look you'll plainly see.

There's nature's beauty all around
It's in the air and on the ground,
Fall's abundance, easily found,
And it's there to see for free.

Autumn's painted on every tree,
Nature's beautiful leaf marquee,
Colorful corner canopy.

The Streets of St. Paul are very colorful in the fall, as this section of the book can attest. This particular corner shows a bit of everything, as I noted in the poem.

This poem is a Zejel.

ZEJEL: A Spanish form. The first stanza, known as the mudanza, has three lines, rhyming aaa. All other stanzas, as many as you like, have 4 lines, with the rhyme going back to the first stanza. So as you read, you are pulled back to those first rhymes sounds, regardless of the other rhymes that inhabit a stanza. Of course, those are akin to mono-rhyme, until you are carried back again and again. Rhyme Scheme:

aaa bbba ccca ddda etc.

Colloquial language tends to be used. Meter: 8-syllable lines (not obligatory).

For this poem I also added a closing 3 line Envoi with an aaa rhyme scheme that repeats, and therefor echoes, the first three lines.

Alliteration: colorful corner canopy, arrayed autumn, season's style show, be beat, such sight see, are also, walks we, jump joyously, so serene, Air and, Fall's found, there to, for free.

Metaphor: Autumn's painted, leaf marquee, canopy, season's style show.

Personification: Tree limbs arching, colors blaze.

Caesura: stanza 5, Line 3.

This photograph was taken by the author in September of 2012, in the Cathedral area,

Poem #12

AUTUM'S GOLDEN VEIL
(A Sonnet)

What golden droplets fall from Autumn's veil,
To drape in brilliant color 'cross this trail,
For shoes to shuffle slowly through them all,
A pleasure that's unique to only Fall.

These blended hues provide a gorgeous sight,
When orange and yellow tinges first ignite
To make the yards and neighborhoods invite
The passersby to marvel with delight.

Then OH, how very wonderful it feels
To have the leaflets crunch beneath our heels,
To blow in swirling whirlpools in the breeze,
As colors clothe those staying in the trees.

So, let me walk within this glowing splendor
That only finest artisans could render.

The Fall colors where truly spectacular this year, as this sidewalk scene clearly shows. The oranges and yellows were particularly vivid. I couldn't get enough of them. My camera was busy capturing it all. This walk along the river trail was inspiring.

This poem is a Sonnet.

A traditional sonnet is a poem of 14 lines. It follows a strict rhyme scheme. It is often about love.

A Shakespearean, or English, sonnet consists of 14 lines, each line containing ten syllables and written in iambic pentameter, in which a pattern of an unstressed syllable followed by a stressed syllable is repeated five times. The rhyme scheme in a Shakespearean sonnet is:

a-b-a-b, c-d-c-d, e-f-e-f, g-g;

while an English Sonnet will typically rhyme using coupled rhyme, as this:

aabb ccdd eeff gg.

So this is an English Sonnet.

The last two lines, in this poem, are a rhyming couplet, which contains feminine iambic pentameter. That is an acceptable convention in an iambic line. It adds one extra syllable count with a soft accent. This creates a line of 11 syllables. When feminine iambic meter is employed, it is coupled with another feminine line to create a pair.

Metaphor: autumn's veil.

Hyperbole: see line 9.

Alliteration: color 'cross, shoes shuffle slowly, through them, colors clothe, walk within.

Elision: 'cross.

Onomatopoeia: crunch

This photograph was taken by the author along the East River Road in St. Paul, Minnesota where the homes stretch along the eastern bluffs of the Mississippi River.

Delighted by the color of the leaves, I was out walking in the autumn splendor. There in the tree next to me, a squirrel stood, frozen in an alert position. No doubt, caused by my close proximity. It stayed there in that pose while I snapped this shot. The trees, the leaves, the squirrel, all transpired to inspire this piece. No Cathedral could inspire me more.

This poem is a Rondeau.

A Rondeau is a fixed form of poetry. It is often used in light or witty poems. It often has fifteen octo - or decasyllabic lines with three stanzas. Here I used iambic tetrameter. It usually only has two rhymes (an "a" and a "b" rhyme) used in the poem.

A word or words from the first part of the first line are used as a refrain ending the second and third stanzas, which gives it a lovely echo effect.

The rhyme scheme of a Rondeau is:

aabba aabR aabbaR, where the R represents the repeated word or phrase.

I modified it a bit, giving it a repeating line (just for effect), shown by a capital A. So the rhyme scheme becomes:

aabba AabR aabbAR, where the Capital letters represent repeated lines.

Alliteration: their trunks, as an arch, stunning sight.

Metaphor: trunks are highways, color dome, trees ignite.

Simile: as lovely as an arch.

In-line Rhyme: these trees.

Caesura: line 8.

Enjambment: Lines 4-5

This photograph was taken by the author in October, 2014.

Poem #13

THESE GOLDEN TREES
(A Rondeau)

These golden trees provide a home.
Their trunks are highways squirrels roam,
with leaves ablaze in golden light.
They search the ground, both day and night
for seeds and nuts in fertile loam.

The branches form a color dome,
as lovely as an arch in Rome,
of yellow leaves. A stunning sight -
these golden trees.

No manmade gilded Hippodrome,
or literary written tome,
can match the grandeur of the sight,
when Nature's Autumn trees ignite.
The branches form a color dome.
These golden trees!

CHAPTER 3: BIRDS

· ·

Birds are magnificent in their varying size, color of plumage, diversity of habits and habitats. Creatures of the air, trees, grasses and waters that never cease to fascinate. Great subjects for the poet's muse and the photographer's eye. Whether at the feeder or in the air they brighten our days with action and sound. They may delight us or awe us. Still or in motion, they are wonderful creatures that grace our lives.

Poem #14

A BIRD IN THE HAND
(A Modified Tanka Suite)

A bird in the hand,
Is it worth two in the bush?
With talons THIS sharp,
Upon such soft supple stand,
You might want to wear thick gloves!

A Kestrel's talons
Are a raptor's wicked tool,
Have hard sharpened ends.
So follow all safety rules.
They don't suffer any fools.

Lovely little birds
Like the Eagles, hunt their prey.
These pretty killers,
Colorful as Parakeets,
They are gorgeous on display.

A picture of an American Kestrel taken by the author at a Raptor show. This bird is a member of the Falcon family. It is the most common falcon in North America, and is found in a wide variety of habitats. At 19–21 cm (7–8 in) long, it is also the smallest. It hunts by hovering in the air with rapid wing beats or perching and scanning the ground for prey. Its diet typically consists of grasshoppers, lizards, mice, and small birds (e.g. sparrows). It nests in cavities in trees, cliffs, buildings, and other structures. One important use of American Kestrels is in falconry. It is often considered a beginner's bird. Its colors are striking, as seen here.

This poem is made up of Tankas.

A Tanka is a Japanese format that keys on syllable count. Typically it is a five line poem with a syllable count of: 5-7-5-7-7. There is no meter requirement. Tankas focus on the art of poetic observation and comment. They don't typically use rhyme, capitalization, punctuation, or alliteration, but I modified mine to include some. So, it has been Americanized here. The rhyme scheme is:

abcad efgff hijki.

The first two lines are an example of Colloquialism.

I used capital letters to emphasize a point.

Alliteration: talons this, soft supple stand, want wear, have hard, so safety, lovely little.

Caesura: line 12.

Metaphor: wicked tool.

Personification: they don't suffer any fools

A Question, draws the reader into a poem, by making them a part, by thinking of an answer.

This picture was taken by the author on September 17, 2012.

Poem #15

CEDAR WAXWING
(A Kyrielle Poem)

Lovely what warm weather can bring,
New growth blooms in each tiny sprig,
Upon it perched portent of spring,
A Cedar Waxwing sits on twig.

Small grey bird Is wearing a mask,
Yellow pintails I really dig.
It completes its berry search task,
A Cedar Waxwing sits on twig.

It's a clever colorful bird.
Over water it'll zag and zig.
It's high whistling sound can be heard,
A Cedar Waxwing sits on twig.

The cedar waxwing (Bombycilla cedrorum) is a member of the Waxwing family of passerine birds. Cedar Waxwings fly at 40 km/h (25 mph), and fly at an altitude of 610 m (2,000 ft.). Cedar waxwings are also known as the Southern Waxwing, Canada Robin, Cedar Bird, Cherry Bird, or Recellet. A Lovely bird that eats fruits, berries, and insects. It chases insects over water just like a Starling. Always on the search for berries, it can sit on a twig, or hover like a humming bird. Its song is more like a whistle. Waxwings are attracted to the sound of running water, and love to bathe in and drink from shallow creeks. In urban environments, you'll see them in puddles and birdbaths. Cedar waxwings are sociable, seen in flocks year round. They are non-territorial birds, and will often groom each other. Its fondness for the small cones of the eastern redcedar (a kind of juniper) gave this bird its common name. They eat berries whole. Source: Wikipedia.

This poem is a Kyrielle.

A Kyrielle is made of Quatrains that rhyme. Each stanza (that is a quatrain) has a line that repeats a line from a previous stanza. That line usually (but does not necessarily have to) be the last line in the stanza. Each line in the poem has eight syllables. There is no limit to the number of stanzas. There is no meter requirement. Usually there are three or more stanzas.

Any type of rhyme scheme can be used. Here I used:

abaB cbcB dbdB.

The capital letters show the repeated lines.

Aliteration: what warn weather, perched portent, clever colorful, zig zag.

Poem #16

CROW ASSOCIATION
(Septets)

I heard a crow caw once,
Then twice again.
A grating sound that seems to bounce
As it echoed through the glen.
A somber sound,
Which I've found
Reminded me of troubled times back then.

A time when passion's race was free
To fly unfettered when
The moment struck and danced so merrily.
Back before it began,
Malicious madness,
Sickly sadness,
As birds became unknowing talismen.

For what but evil conspired to take away
The passion we once had to sow
When cruelly lost one fateful day
That started with the calling of a crow.
Awakening to find
Recesses of her mind
Were twisted into someone I didn't know.

It's hard to know what's locked inside the brain
Invisible until the symptoms show.
Lucidity too difficult to obtain,
Typical reactions become slow,
A poignant pain,
A harsh refrain,
Began the day I heard the calling of the crow.

Just a fictional Poem about Alzheimer's disease. I was sitting having my coffee in the morning, when I heard a crow caw. Well, off my Muse went. From whence this came, I know not. But I hope you enjoy it.

A crow is a bird of the genus Corvus. In medieval times, crows were thought to live abnormally long lives. They were also thought to be monogamous throughout their long lives. They were thought to predict the future, to predict rain and reveal ambushes. Crows were also thought to lead flocks of storks while they crossed the sea to Asia. As a group, crows show remarkable examples of intelligence. Natural history books from the 18th century recount an often-repeated, anecdote of "counting crows" — a crow with ability to count to five (or four in some versions). Crows and ravens often score very highly on intelligence tests. Crow is a trickster, culture hero, and ancestral being. Legends relating to Crow have been observed in various groups and cultures; these commonly include stories relating to Crow's role in the theft of fire, the origin of death, and the killing of Eagle's son. A group of Crows is called a Murder.

Source Wikipedia.

This poem is a series of Septets.

A septet is a poem with seven lines. For this one I chose a rhyme scheme of:

ababccb.

There is a variable meter.

Alliteration: crow caw, then twice, sound seems, somber sound, troubled times then, moment merrily, struck so, back before began, malicious madness, sickly sadness, birds became, symptoms show, poignant pain.

Onomatopoeia: caw

I used Flashback and Onomatopoeia as poetic techniques.

The author took this photograph, then modified it with framing.

Poem #17

EAGLE
(A Pleiades Poem)

Eagle, majestic master of top height,
Elegantly swooping, first left, then right,
Each movement a dance step in open sky,
Every wing beat matched with a high-pitched cry
Eerily sounding in the mountain air.
Exquisite symbol of freedom we share,
Evoking Emotion, Power, and Might.

Poem about an Eagle inspired by my photograph and another Poet on my poetry site.

This is a Pleiades Poem.

A Pleiades poem has a title with a single word. The poem itself has seven lines. The first word in each line begins with the same letter as the title. A poetry form created by Craig Tigerman, there is no syllable count or rhyme scheme requirement. However, not a very difficult style to achieve. I thought that this format was too simple and tame, so I added some challenge to it.

For this poem I chose a syllable count with pentameter (10 syllables). I chose a rhyme scheme of:

aabbcca.

Alliteration: majestic master, strep sky, evoking emotion.

Capitalization to create impact of the words.

Kinesthesia: swooping left then right, wing beat matched.

Metaphor: dance step, symbol of freedom

Personification: movement a dance step.

Onomatopoeia: high-pitched cry

This picture of an eagle was taken on October 2012 at Fort Snelling State Park along the river bottoms of the Mississippi River in Minnesota just below the Minneapolis, St. Paul International Airport. The bridge in the background is the Highway I35E bridge.

This picture moved me to write this poem in conjunction with inspiration from the poem I reviewed on 2/5/2013, called The Eagle, by Robin Gilmor.

Poem #18

LANDING GOOSE
(A Shardoma Poem)

Landing fast,
A Canada goose
Streaking past.
I'm aghast!
With that splashing water cast,
Landing gear let loose
Canada
May be in your name
You're kinda
Quite fonda
The grasses of Bermuda
that's your claim to fame.

Wish you'd stayed
In north wilderness
But you strayed
To invade
Our parks with messes you made
To such great excess.

Skimming the water as it lands, a Canada Goose in action. The Canada Goose (Branta canadensis) is a large wild Goose species with a black head and neck, white patches on the face, and a brown body. Native to arctic and temperate regions of North America, its migration occasionally reaches northern Europe. The Canada Goose is the most common Goose found in Minnesota. So much so, that they have become a nuisance. Extremely successful at living in human-altered areas, Canada Geese have proven able to establish breeding colonies in urban and cultivated areas, which provide food and few natural predators, and are well known as a common park species. Canada Goose populations in some areas have grown substantially, so much so that many consider them pests for their droppings, bacteria in their droppings, noise, and confrontational behavior. Canada geese are primarily herbivores, although they sometimes eat small insects and fish. Their diet includes green vegetation and grains. The Canada Goose eats a variety of grasses when on land. It feeds by grasping a blade of grass with the bill, then tearing it with a jerk of the head. Source: Wikipedia.

This poem is a Shardoma.

A Shardoma is a short poem of six lines (a sextet) with a fixed syllable count of:

3/5/3/3/7/5.

This gives it a lively, expressive tempo. It can either be free verse or rhymed.

I chose to rhyme it. I used:

abaaab.

A Shardoma may have more than one stanza.

Alliteration: landing loose,

Diction: kinda, fonda (a folksy use of language).

Hyperbola: I'm agast.

In-line rhyme: claim fame

Kinesthesia: landing fast, streaking past

I took this photograph on the Mississippi, at Grey Cloud Island near Cottage Grove, Minnesota, with my Sony Alpha, high speed camera. This is one frame from a 20 frame sequence.

Poem #19

PILEATED WOODPECKERS
(Mixed Poetry Styles)

Watched these shadows fly
Past windowpane they went by
Black with two bright heads

Red tufted
Pileated breed
Peck for feed

On family fence, these creatures alight,
Big birds with colors black and white.
Crested head shows blazing red,
And pointed beak to dread.
In this neighborhood,
Tearing up wood,
Folks foresee,
Would be
Bad.

Red
Crested,
White chested,
Long pointed beak
Gets hard wood bark bested
With a sharp jackhammer head tweak.
Gains instant access toward insects they seek.
Hope to keep them away from my house, fence, or shed
Once there on my roof, it could spring a leak.
Best they stay on trees by the creek,
Where they all once nested.
With skilled technique,
Once rested,
Lifted.
Fled.

Fence
Woodpeckers that go whence
Tense

These two Pileated Woodpeckers landed on the fence in my backyard. I'm happy they didn't start chewing up my cedar fence. They are the largest woodpeckers in North America. It was great to see them and catch a picture, but I'm glad they didn't stay long. They belong in the forest.

For this poem, I used several styles of poetry. I started with 5-7-5 followed by 3-5-3. Then I went to a Nonet, followed by a Diatelle. I closed with a 1-6-1 style. The 5-7-5, 3-5-3, and 1-6-1 Poems are all driven by the named syllable count.

A Nonet is a nine line poem. The first line containing nine syllables, the next line has eight syllables, the next line has seven syllables. That continues until the last line (the ninth line) which has one syllable. Nonets can be written about any subject. Rhyming is optional. A perfect Nonet is centered and the structure forms a nice V shape. If right justified, it should make a nice inverted staircase.

A Diatelle was created by Bradley Vrooman and has a set syllable count and a set rhyme.

Syllable count is: 1-2-3-4-6-8-10-12-10-8-6-4-3-2-1,

The rhyme patter is: abbcbccaccbcbba.

It is usually displayed centered to make a diamond shaped structure.

This picture was a photograph taken by the author.

Poem #20

WHITE IN FLIGHT
(Free Form)

I watched
as it rose from the water
in an explosion
of feathers and froth.
It skimmed
the forest edge
along the wave tops
and
majestically lifted into the blue
circling above my head
as I fumbled
to
get the lens on it.
And then,
as quickly as he had come,
he was
gone

This is a Free Form word sculpt about an event that included a startle and then quick reaction to achieve the resulting photograph. A look into the photographer's plight while still marveling at nature's beauty.

The bird is a Great White Egret.

The Great White Egret (Ardea alba), is also known as the Common Egret, Large Egret or Great White Heron. The scientific name comes from Latin ardea "heron", and alba, "white." It is a large heron with all-white plumage. Standing up to 1 m (3.3 ft) tall, this species can measure 80 to 104 cm (31 to 41 in) in length and have a wingspan of 131 to 170 cm (52 to 67 in). Apart from size, the great egret can be distinguished from other white egrets by its yellow bill and black legs and feet. It has a slow flight, with its neck retracted. This is characteristic of herons and bitterns, and distinguishes them from storks, cranes, ibises, and spoonbills, which extend their necks in flight. In North America, large numbers of great egrets were killed around the end of the 19th century so that their plumes could be used to decorate hats. Numbers have since recovered as a result of conservation measures.

This poem is Free Style.

A Free Style Poem is a subset of Free Verse. It has no rhyme scheme, tempo, or meter pattern. It just flows with the words. The author adds dimension in how the poem is felt, through the use of pace and pause, created in how the words are arranged on the page. The distinction between Free Style and Free Verse is that Free Style contains some rhyme while Free Verse does not. It rhymes in places as the author wants, but not necessarily consistently.

Alliteration: feathers froth.

Poetic Imagery was used throughout.

I also used Kinesthesia quite a bit.

This photograph was taken by the author himself at Battle Creek Park in Maplewood Minnesota.

CHAPTER 4: FLOWERS

For overall beauty, it is hard to beat the flower. Such variety of size, shape and color is a poet's as well as photographer's dream. Some have been beautifully cultured and domesticated. Others are wildflowers. There's even the lowly weed. All of them are unique and exquisite. This chapter gives the reader a sampling of each.

Poem #21

BITTERSWEET NIGHTSHADE
(A Poem about a Wildflower)

Nightshade: a bittersweet
Wildflower you may meet.

When Bittersweet Nightshade hangs on the vine
Its attractive colors may look divine.
With pretty purple flowers on narrow stem,
So clearly centered on bright yellow shoots,
May attract curious children to them.
Beware of tiny red poisonous fruits!

Nightshade: a bittersweet
Wildflower you may meet.

When Bittersweet Nightshade hangs on the vine
Its creepers may climb to choke a small pine.
An invasive plant, survives any clime,
While its leaves can cause an itchy rash too,
It out-competes native shrubs most the time,
So it's a problem for folks to walk through.

Nightshade: a bittersweet
Wildflower you may meet.

When Bittersweet Nightshade hangs on the vine
You don't even want to feed it to swine.
It needs very little sunshine or care.
It can grow in a field, forest, or street.
In fact, it can grow almost anywhere.
Bittersweet Nightshade: wildflower you may meet.

So it may look pretty
In forest or city,
If it's found in your zone
Best leave it alone.

This wildflower can be dangerous. It is called Bittersweet Nightshade, but is has also been called: Blue Bindweed, Climbing Nightshade, Poisonberry, Snakeberry, and Violet Bloom. It has a pretty purple flower around a yellow stamen. It is native to Asia, Northern Africa, and Europe, but is invasive to North America. It is related to the potato and the tomato. It has a red berry that is poisonous to livestock and humans, but is a food to some birds, especially the Thrushes. The fruits and leaves contain Solanine. The fruit changes colors as it matures from green, to yellow, to orange, and then to red. The leaves and immature berries are the most toxic and have been known to kill children. You can also get a rash from the leaves and stems. It is considered a noxious weed in many states in the US.

It grows in all terrains, especially wetlands and forests, but does fine on roadsides, even in cities. Its vines can out-compete most native shrubs. It can overgrow and choke out small trees.

This poem has no formal format. The large stanzas have a rhyme scheme of:

aabcbc

and syllable count of 10.

The envoi has a rhyme scheme of aabb and syllable count of 6.

The refrains are rhyming couplets with a count of 6.

Alliteration: may meet, pretty purple, clearly centered chutes, curious children, creepers climb choke, can cause, for folks, field forest.

Metaphor: look divine,

Personification: choke a pine

Warning: beware of tiny red fruits, Best leave it alone.

This photograph is one of the author's collection. It was actually taken by his grandson, Jeremy T Hamlin.

Poem #22

BURSTING BLOOM
(Mixed Stanzas)

It comes to me as such a shock
such beauty grows atop this stalk.
Reminds me of the color burst
as firework fragments first dispersed
to light the darkest ev'ning skies.
So too, this bloom seems to my eyes.

Big petals bend to grasp the air
which gives this bloom a frantic flair,
combining with true color hue,
to yield a most enticing view.

I wonder what this blossom is,
since I am not a flower wiz.
Yet, doesn't matter anyway.
I still enjoy its bright display,
and that's OK.

This orange colored flower is one of several that I encountered along the path at the Arboretum. The way its petals spread, reminded me of a fireworks burst in the sky. I believe those are also referred to as "blooms". So I used that correlation for this poem.

This poem used a mixed set of stanzas, although I held the iambic tetrameter constant. The first verse has 6 lines (a Sestet). The second has 4 lines (a Quatrain). The third one has 5 lines - the Quintrain.

The overall rhyme scheme is: aabbcc ddee ffggg.

Alliteration: such shock, firework fragments first, to this to, big bends, frantic flair, combining color, wonder what.

Caesura: line 6, and 14.

In-line Rhyme: true hue, this is.

Folksy Language: I wonder, flower wiz, that's OK.

Personification: grasp the air.

Simile: as fireworks fragments disperse.

Elision: ev'ning

I took this macro photograph on October 17, 2014 with my Sony Alpha camera.

Poem #23

HEART OF FIRE
(A Quatern Poem)

There's beauty in a heart of fire
Producing bright visions that glow.
Beauty outside creates desire.
But, what's glowing inside will show.

It's those with great wisdom who know,
There's beauty in a heart of fire.
When kindled with love it will grow.
Tending, it will never require.

Rose's petals, you may admire,
They delicately curl and flow.
There's beauty in a heart of fire.
As you gaze, it's where eyes will go.

Looking outside, you'll never know,
"Till you see what centers inspire.
The inner space you must follow.
There's beauty in a heart of fire.

This Rose certainly has one. When I saw this rose, the first line immediately came to mind.

The poem is a Quatern.

The Quatern is a French form of poetry that is composed of four quatrains, (four-line stanzas). It is similar to the Kyrielle and other French poems, in that it has a repeated refrain. But, unlike other French forms, it doesn't have to rhyme--there is no rhyme scheme specified. Similar to other French forms of poetry, the Quatern consists of lines with eight syllables each, and has no required meter. The Refrain starts as the first line of the first Stanza, then the second line of the second, the third of the third, and the last line of the fourth stanza. So it moves through the poem in a cascade.

Even though they do not have to rhyme or follow a specific meter, I have chosen to write my Quatern poems in tetrameter, but not iambic, with a rhyme scheme of:

Abab, bAba, abAb, babA,

where the first and third lines of each stanza rhyme and where the second and fourth lines of each stanza rhyme, and the A represents the Refrain line.

Alliteration: with wisdom who, when with will, where will.

Caesura: line 4, 8, 9, 12, 13

Elision: 'til.

Metaphor: fire, kindle, tending.

I mostly used poetic imagery here.

This picture was taken by the author at the Lake Harriet Rose Garden in Minneapolis, Minnesota..

Poem #24

LIVELY LILY
(A Triolet)

When lively Lily brightly shines
It gives a mellow yellow tone,
Amongst its leaves it deftly climbs.
When lively Lily brightly shines,
In masterful floral designs,
Its quiet beauty stands alone,
When lively Lily brightly shines
It gives a mellow yellow tone.

This Lily, that I spotted while out on a walk with my wife, appeared to be grasping and climbing its leaves. So, I made reference to that in this poem.

This poem is a Triolet.

A Triolet is a poem with a fixed format. This one has a syllable structure of 8 counts or tetrameter. It is a poem of only eight lines with a rhyme scheme of only two rhymes (a and b) that can be represented as follows:

ABaAabAB,

where the fourth and seventh lines are the same exact line as the first. The eighth line is the same exact line as the second (This is represented by the capital letters shown). So, it is very important to compose the first two lines carefully so that the entire poem flows well and is enhanced by the repeats.

Alliteration: lively lily.

In-line Rhyme: mellow yellow.

Hyperbole: masterful floral designs

Personification: it climbs

The photograph is one the author took himself.

Poem #25

O LOVELY FLOWERS
(Swap Quatrains)

Your bounty overflows, in bulging flower pot,
With rich diversity in colors that it shows,
And all the many types of flowered plants it's wrought.
In bulging flower pot, your bounty overflows.

We are truly blessed with a world full of colors.
The Creator has put them here, you may have guessed.
A flower transforms environments it alters.
With a world full of colors, we are truly blessed.

O lovely Flowers

With red and yellow blooms, they brighten walks and rooms,
Along with pink, purple, white in delicate plumes,
All wafting with the lovely scent of sweet perfumes,
They brighten walks and rooms with red and yellow blooms.

Lying on lovely seas of green, in pots of clay.
Placed by the gardener's gentle hand, in sweet bouquet
Deftly arranged to please, in artistic display
In pots of clay, lying on seas of green.

O lovely flowers

They transform any environment. A pot of lovely flower on a sidewalk makes a lovely statement, and dresses up even the plainest concrete. These were on the walkway from the parking lot into the Como Conservatory, in St. Paul, Minnesota.

This poem is formatted with Swap Quatrains.

Swap quatrains are verses of four lines where the two halves of the first line is swapped in reverse order with the two halves of the fourth (basically line 1 and 4 are the same, only reversed). To accommodate that flip-flop, the lines need to have 10, 12, 14, or 16 syllables.

The rhyme scheme of the first quatrain is abab. Do not repeat the same rhyme pattern in subsequent stanzas. So, the full rhyme scheme of this poem is:

abab cded ffff gggh.

Alliteration: bounty bulging, with world we, has here have, blooms brighten, pink purple plumes, wafting with, scent sweet, lying lovely, gardener's gentle, deftly display.

Carsura: line 1, 4, 6, 8, 10, 11, 14,15,16, 17.

In-line Rhyme: blooms rooms.

Folksy Language: you may have guessed.

I also added a repeated refrain.

Poem #26

ORANGE ON GOLD
(Swap Quatrains)

Orange upon gold, floral delight,
Blooms are such a beautiful sight.
Glorious glow, petals unfold,
Floral delight, orange upon gold.

Travel around. See what you see,
Awesome views around the city.
Season's height means colors abound.
See what you see. Travel around.

Flower planted in fertile fields,
Creates the glories nature yields.
Shrewd sown seeds, don't take for granted
In fertile fields, flowers planted.

Orange on gold takes your breath away.
A showy scene that gods portray,
Beguiled be, by a sight so bold.
Takes your breath away, orange on gold.

Another beautiful flower grouping I caught at the Lake Harriet Rose Gardens in Minneapolis. I searched profusely to find out what kind of flowers these may be, but couldn't identify them. The closest I could get, was some kind of exotic Zinnia.

This poem is another format introduced to me creatively by Gungalo, in her poem, The Skirt. It is called Swap Quatrains.

This poem is formatted with Swap Quatrains.

Swap quatrains are verses of four lines where the two halves of the first line is swapped in reverse order with the two halves of the fourth (basically line 1 and 4 are the same, only reversed). To accommodate that flip-flop, the lines need to have 10, 12, 14, or 16 syllables.

The rhyme scheme of the first quatrain is abab. Do not repeat the same rhyme pattern in subsequent stanzas. However, I held that original pattern throughout. So, the full rhyme scheme of this poem is:

AABB CCDD and so on.

Alliteration: glorious glow, see see, awesome around, shrewd sown seed, fertile fields flowers, showy scene, beguiled be by bold.

Caesura: 1, 4, 7, 8, 11, 12.

Exhortation: see what you see, travel around, don't take for granted.

Metaphor, scene that gods portray.

This picture was taken by the author himself.

Poem #27

PINK COSMOS FLOWER
(Modified Octogram)

Pretty petals stretch to the sky.
The Pink Cosmos!
On delicate stem that captures the eye,
There may be pathos.
When battered by hard wind or rain,
Its broken bough may not regain
The strength these beauties must retain.
The Pink Cosmos.

In Greek, called Balanced Universe,
In the pasture.
To the south, it's known to be the diverse
Mexican Aster.
There's beauty there you can't deny,
Attracting bees and butterfly,
With hues that truly gratify.
The Pink Cosmos.

In this one, I tried to define this lovely plant, with its delicate stem. This flower is known as a Cosmos. It is part of my wild flower series as I found it growing in the wild. It comes in several species and colors. This one is Cosmos Bipinatus, which is also known as the Mexican Aster. The name Cosmos in Greek, means Balanced Universe, derived from its delicate narrow stem and thin leaves that grow out equally on both sides of the stem to help it balance (much like a tight-rope walker's balance pole does). However, this comes at a price, as this flower can easily be damaged by high winds or heavy rains. This flower is native to Mexico, but can be grown almost anywhere. It is usually a garden flower. Those growing in the wild are typically garden escapees. Its close cousin, the Cosmos Caudatus grows in Indonesia and Malaysia. There it is considered a health food, as the leaves and stems are used in salads. It contains Awet Muda, with anti-aging properties that tones up the blood, strengthens the bones, and freshens breath. Its American cousin is only considered an ornamental plant.

This is modified from the structure of an Octogram.

The Octogram is a style of poetry invented by Fanstorian Sally Yocom (S.Yocom). It consists of two stanzas of eight lines each, with a very specific syllable count and rhyme scheme.

Syllable count is 84848884, repeat on second stanza.

I modified that to 8/4/10/5/8/8/8/4.

The typical Rhyme scheme: aBabccbB ababddbB, where B repeats same text.

I modified that too, to: aBabcccB dedeaabB.

Alliteration: pretty petals, stretch sky, battered by, broken bough, bees butterfly.

Caesura: line 9 and 11.

Enjambment: lines 6 to 7, 11 to 12.

Personification: captures the eye.

This picture was taken by the author himself along the shoreline of Lake McCarron, in St. Paul, Mn.

Poem #28

PURPLE VETCH
(Quatrains with Closing Couplet)

Stumbled upon some purple vetch,
Walking along a parkway stretch
That was blazoned with wildflowers,
Purple and yellow - watched for hours.

Stopped to behold this nature's treat,
There to enjoy, right at my feet,
Beautiful bells draped on a vine,
Imperial purple - Divine!

Nestled near it, a yellow cup.
I hastened to look, close up.
To my surprise, what did I see?
A Canada Anemone!

With wildflowers like these, we are blessed!
These days when we find them are - The Best!

Some more wildflowers that I photographed on my walk with my wife.

The purple flower in the picture is Purple Vetch. Vetch is one of the oldest known cultivated plants in the world. It is part of the green bean or legume family and related to lentils and peas. According to Wikipedia, Vetch was known in the Near East 9,500 years ago. It has been found in Neolithic sites in Bulgaria, Hungary, and Slovakia, about 7,000 years ago. St. Bernard of Clairvaux shared bread of vetch meal with his monks during the famine of 1124-1126. They were mentioned in the Hebrew bible. It was replaced by better plants like wheat and corn. Today, it is used, if at all, as forage, but is mostly considered an invasive weed.

The Canada Anemone is the little yellow flower in the picture. It is a perennial that grows with horizontal underground roots (rhizomes). Native Americans considered it to have many medicinal uses, such as a styptic for wounds, an eyewash, and for many other ailments.

This poem is a set of three Quatrains with a closing rhyming couplet. The rhyme scheme for the quatrains is abab with a syllable count of 8. The closing couplet is a simple end rhyme with a syllable count of 9. Some lines are trochaic, others iambic, others are anapestic. Because of the mixed meter and unusual 9 count of the couplet, I didn't call this a Sonnet, although it has a similar structure.

Alliteration: stumbled some, beautiful bells, nestled near, surprise see, with wildflowers we, when we.

Caesura: line 4, 6, 8, 9, 10, 11.

Kinesthesia: stumbled upon, walking along, stopped, hastened to look

Hyperbole: blazoned with, divine

Metaphor: nature's treat, beautiful bells,

Personification: nestled near it.

Question: what did I see?

The photograph was taken by me on June 24, 2013.

Poem #29

RAINDROPS ON FLOWERS
(A Modern Sonnet)

Love the raindrops on the flowers
In summer early morning hours
that moistened both petal and leaf
In suddenly sodden motif

Soon a kiss from heated sunlight
That will undoubtedly alight
Shall dazzle glistening dewdrops
As they linger on blossom tops

Then will the vegetation dance
Draped in ornamental romance
Within their green garden domains
On feeling gentle summer rains

'Tis just the way of nature's things
The joyousness renewal brings

I love to look at flowers after a summer rain shower, such as this lovely yellow lily. No matter how violent the storm, it brings renewal.

This poem is a Sonnet. It has three quatrains with an aabb rhyme scheme followed by a closing rhyming couplet giving it the required 14 lines. This one is not iambic. I did it in tetrameter. It has a Volta on line 9, as required. Therefore it's mixed tetrameter. Since it is not iambic, it would be classified as a Modern Sonnet. It was intentionally done without punctuation.

Alliteration: suddenly sodden, soon sunlight, dazzle dewdrops, green garden, 'tis the things.

Elision: 'tis

Personification: kiss of sunlight, dewdrops linger, shall dazzle, vegetation dance, feeling rains.

Poetic imagery: suddenly sodden, heated sunlight, draped in romance.

This photograph was taken be the author himself.

CHAPTER 5: INSECTS

· ·

Insects can be beautiful, as the butterfly; strange, like the spider or scorpion; or ugly, like the stink bug. You wouldn't think there's much to be poetic about in this group, but maybe that's not true. The author hopes this chapter will give a better appreciation for the topic and the creatures that are its subject matter.

Poem #30

BUTTERFLY ON THISTLE
*(A Minute Poem)_*

I saw a monarch on a bush
Delicate wings
Color that sings
Of all good things

That butterfly sat on a lush
Branch of thistle
Sticky bristle
Made me whistle

Forgot about my urgent rush
The sight was sweet
It was a treat
My day complete

Just a playful poem.

A pretty Butterfly settled on the path I was rushing by. It landed on a thistle with a pretty purple flower on it. This was a Monarch Butterfly that was sharing a purple thistle with a couple of beetles. So,..you know.

The Monarch Butterfly or simply Monarch (Danaus plexippus) is a milkweed butterfly. Other names include Milkweed, Common Tiger, Wanderer, and Black Veined Brown. The eastern North American Monarch is notable for its annual migration from the United States and southern Canada to Mexico, where Monarchs cover thousands of miles, with a corresponding multi-generational return north. There is increasing concern for the decline of monarchs; based on a twenty-year comparison, the population west of the Rocky Mountains has dropped more than 50 percent since 1997 and east of the Rockies declined by more than 90 percent since 1995.

The U.S. Fish and Wildlife Service provided a statistic showing that nearly a billion monarchs have vanished since 1990. One of the main reasons was herbicides used by farmers and homeowners on milkweed, a plant used as a food source, a home and a nursery by the monarchs.

This poem is a variation on a Minute Poem.

The Minute Poem is a poem that follows the "8,4,4,4" syllable count structure. It usually has 3 stanzas that are exactly the same. So: 8,4,4,4; 8,4,4,4; 8,4,4,4 syllables.

A traditional Minute Poem has 12 lines total. It has 60 syllables. It is written in a strict iambic meter. The rhyme scheme is as follows: aabb, ccdd, eeff.

I deviated from that with a rhyme scheme of abbb accc addd, but it is iambic. Lack of punctuation is intentional.

Alliteration: sight sweet.

Personification and Metaphor: color that sings

This picture is one taken by the author in August 2012.

Poem #31

DRAGONFLY IN FLIGHT

(An 8-8-10 Metered Sestet with closing Envoi)

I watched a dragonfly today
Play in the meadow, near the bay.
It flitted up and down to my delight,
On double wings so delicate
That any learned estimate
Would guess they'd break apart in stress of flight.

Those see-through wings of black and white
That seem so delicate and light
Will carry little dragon on the wind
At speeds to take your breath away
In agile, acrobatic play,
Then hover gracefully where air has thinned.

To look at him, you'd think he'd sting,
Or take a bite of everything,
But that perception simply isn't true.
For he's a helpful little bug,
Not enemy or hurtful thug,
He benefits the places he flies through.

These creatures are misunderstood.
Their habits really are quite good.

They actually will never sting or bite.
These tiny airborne torpedoes
Quickly catch and eat mosquitoes.
For them, they have a healthy appetite.

These acrobats command the sky.
So, when you see a dragonfly,
Appreciate their lovely style and grace.
Just watch how fast it comes and goes,
Then settles on a twig to pose,
And realize its value to this place.

I marvel at its color hues.
It comes in black, and reds, and blues.
While sometimes, there's a purple or a pink.
Near babbling brook, or glim'ring lake,
Is where I find their wings partake
Of currents, flying faster than you'd think.

This one that's spotted black and white,
Is such a delicate delight,
That I could watch its antics all day long.
Would that be wrong?

This dragonfly is known as a 12 Spotted Skimmer. I found it at a nature park in St. Paul, Minnesota. The dragonfly is a very interesting insect. Dragonflies were some of the first winged insects to evolve, some 300 million years ago. Modern dragonflies have wingspans of only two to five inches, but fossil dragonflies have been found with wingspans of up to two feet. There are more than 5,000 known species of dragonflies, all of which (along with damselflies) belong to the order Odonata, which means "toothed one" in Greek and refers to the dragonfly's serrated teeth.

Dragonflies are expert fliers. They can fly straight up and down, hover like a helicopter, and even mate mid-air. If they can't fly, they'll starve, because they only eat prey they catch while flying. Dragonflies, which eat insects as adults, are a great control on the mosquito population. A single dragonfly can eat 30 to hundreds of mosquitoes per day. Several years of their life are spent as a nymph living in freshwater; the adults may be on the wing for just a few days or weeks. They are fast agile fliers, sometimes migrating across oceans, and are often but not always found near water due to the fact that their larvae exist entirely in water. Their presence indicates a clean and healthy water zone. There are old and unreliable claims that dragonflies can fly at up to 60 - 65 miles per hour. That is amazing. There are many myths about Daragonflies. Source: The Smithsonian and Wikipedia.

This poem is structured in Sextets (6 line stanzas). It has a rhyme scheme of aabccb, and a meter of 8-8-10-8-8-10.

In this poem I used alliteration, caesura, metaphor, enjambment, kinesthesia, imagery, elision, and question. I just don't have room here to point them all out. Maybe you?

This photograph was taken by the author himself on June 21, 2012.

CHAPTER 6: GARDEN

What is a garden, but a place of beauty crafted by the hand of mankind? It is a sanctuary, a place of solitude and contemplation, and a place to go and marvel at the colors that abound. Each garden is a masterpiece in its own right. Most have paths and places to sit. Some may have water in pools, fountains, or ponds. All are to be viewed and appreciated. They are natural magnets for the poet and the photographer. This chapter is meant to give a flavor of some.

Poem #32

MY FAVORITE BENCH
(A Rispetto Poem)

My favorite bench is occupied,
And now I know not where to go.
I need some exercise outside,
But where I rest, got filled with snow.

I expect that in this season,
That provides a chilly reason,
A snowmelt may take several weeks.
Guess I'll sit and get frozen cheeks.

OK, maybe I'll bring along a shovel next time.

This poem is a Rispetto.

The Rispetto is a classic Italian form, an 8 line poem in which the rhyme scheme for the first stanza is abab, and then the rhyme for the second stanza changes to ccdd.

Alliteration: snowmelt several.

Caesura: line 4.

Folksy Language: my favorite bench, now I know, guess I'll sit.

Personification: bench is occupied.

Humor: frozen cheeks.

Hyperbole: chilly reason, frozen.

Speaker Technique: My, I know, I need, I expect, I'll sit.

This photograph was taken by the author at a nearby park in January 2012.

Poem #33

SERENITY OF ZEN
(Tri-rhymed Sestets)

The essence of serenity,
Based in reality,
Is a locality
That highlights the beauty around,
Which often can be found
To delight and astound.

It's amazing to find a place
Full of beauty and grace,
A very special space
That blends the best aspects of two
Different points of view
Into what artists imbue.

An Asian architecture blends
Its ancient Bonsai trends,
To yield aesthetic ends,
Which stands in Nature's glen
To bring the likes of men
The qualities of Zen.

And all of this can here be seen
In quiet setting, so serene.

The setting of this photograph, with the Bonsai tree, Asian trestles, stones, and chairs surrounded by natural fall beauty inspired this poem. I tried to describe its essence. I hope you enjoy it.

This poem is a suite of Tri-rhymed Sestets with closing couplet. A Sestet is a poem with six line verses. Here, every 3 lines are mono-rhymed. I have been experimenting with Poems that contain three consecutive rhymes. Here, I also played with meter. Six lines with 2 sets of 3 rhymes, but also Meter that has an 8 syllable line followed by 2 with 6, repeated twice. So, for this poem, the entire rhyme scheme is:

aaabbb cccddd eeefff gg.

The syllable count is:

866866 866866 866866 88.

Alliteration: special space, blends best, an Asian architecture, and all, setting so serene.

Caesura: line 20.

Poetic imagery: essence of serenity, beauty around, beauty and grace, special space, artists imbue, ancient Bonsai trends, qualities of Zen.

Hyperbole: delight and astound, amazing to find, so serene.

This photograph was taken by the author himself in October, 2014 at the Minnesota Arboretum.

CHAPTER 7: PATHWAYS

· ·

As we journey through our lives we walk on many different paths. Some are crossroads. Some take us to the unknown. Others are familiar, well warn, and comforting. Whatever the case, they transition us from here - to there. Here in this chapter I describe a couple that I have found. Join me in this walk.

Poem #34

NATURE
(Free Verse)

*I have always felt close
to Nature.*

*Its Beauty and sheer
Immensity
seem to generate a Warm feeling
of Religious
experience.*

*For what Great Cathedral
or
any Man-made object
could compare with the Evolutional
Works
of God?*

*When I am in a natural setting:
be it Glassy Clear Lake,
or Mountain;
Rolling Plain or Billowing Sky;
the Overwhelming Feeling that is
my
personal Experience,
Is one of Celestial Quiet
And Peace.*

*The greatest feeling of Awe
comes at night,*

*Sitting in front of a Crackling Fire;
listening to the Evening Sounds;
an Insect Serenade,
while
staring up into the Vast Dark Universe,
through
layers of Twinkling Stars
that seem to*

*go on
Forever.*

*When I look up at that sky,
through
Row upon Row
of
Tall and Stately
trees,
it is Difficult to Comprehend
that,
although man can travel through Space,
Searching the Stars
for the Secrets of the Universe,
he cannot understand
the
Natural Order
surrounding
him.*

*When I walk through the woods,
kicking leaf
after
Fragile Leaf
from my path;
Breathing Deeply of the cold
Invigorating
air;
I can see the forest
Teeming
with Uncomplicated
Purposeful
life.*

*I can touch the rough
Gnarled Bark*

*of
Sturdy
tree trunks,
grown old with Grace
and
Sovereign Dignity.*

*I can smell
the Mingled Fragrances of flowers,
and honey,
and Uncut Grass,*

*that
Grow Wild along the path,
ignored by the Hurried Passing
of Man.*

**I can hear the Babbling Brook
as
it winds
its Icy Way
down
the mountain,
and drops its Last Few Feet
into the ocean's
Pounding Surf.*

*I can see the Rainbow of colors
reflected in a delicate flower's
petals,
and the Exposed Layers of the
Grand Canyon.*

*For
beauty can be seen Everywhere
for those who take the Time
to Look.*

Poem #35

SUCH A DAY
(Blank Verse Sonnet)

Delight in such a lovely autumn day!
It's wonderful to go, to be outside.
Decide to walk, or jog, or just to sit,
Absorbing classic color on the trees.

Where gentle breezes blow, and birds may sing,
Content amongst the foliage, so serene.
We dream to come and sit on benches there,
And calmly watch the world go drifting by.

Here cyclists can stop to take a rest,
While avid jogger finds a ready path.
Two lovers sit and chat adoringly
As filtered sunlight dapples leaves on grass.

It's swell, and all is well on such a day,
When autumn leaves have turned where people dwell.

This image suggests the Poem. Therefore, its descriptions are Ekphrastic. This scene was taken along the pathway that parallels the Mississippi River Boulevard. This is the east bank of the river, so it is the St. Paul side. The west bank also has a Boulevard but it is in Minneapolis. Besides the jogger, notice the long shadows, the biker on one bench, and the couple on the other. Not to mention the autumn colors. Hopefully the print resolution is good enough.

This poem is a Blank Verse Sonnet,

A Blank Verse Sonnet encompasses two poetic formats blended into one – Blank Verse and a Sonnet.

Blank Verse is a poem written in iambic pentameter, but without any rhyme. Sonnets are usually written in iambic pentameter, but has one of several strict rhyme schemes. An English, or Shakespearian Sonnet is usually written with abab rhymed quatrains and a closing rhymed couplet, for a total of 14 lines. This format blends both using the structure of the Sonnet, but with the elimination of rhyme of the Blank Verse. Therefore is relies heavily in other poetic techniques.

Alliteration: delight day, to go to be, jog just, classic color, breezes blow birds, so serene, watch world, cyclists can, to take, and all, when where.

Caesura: line 2,3, 5,6, 11.

Hyperbole: it's wonderful, so serene, we dream, avid jogger, adoringly

Kinesthesia: walk, jog, sit, breezes blow, come and sit, take a rest,

Poetic imagery: absorbing classic color, gentle breezes blow, birds sing, calmly watch, drifting by, two lovers sit, filtered sunlight dapples,

Onomatopoeia: birds may sing, chat

Woe is me, I couldn't resist a flurry of rhyme in the closing couplet. Dang! Well I tried.

Author's photograph taken October2014.

Poem #36

YELLOW TULIPS

(Decuian)

It's almost having sunlight at your feet,
with yellow tulips growing in the spring.
Among the early flowers, they're elite,
like golden cups on tables of a king.
They lift to capture moisture mornings bring,
in tepals colorful and so petite,
yet giving graceful glow to everything.
The Netherlands have long embraced this flower,
but dogs and cats must never it devour.
We humans are enamored by its power.

I spotted these yellow Tulips, and just had to get a picture of them. This was at Lakewood Cemetery, near Lake Harriet in Minneapolis Minnesota. We went there on Mother's Day to visit my wife, Karen's mother. She died January 17, 2015.

Tepal is- the petal of a tulip.

The tulip is a perennial, bulbous plant in the lily family. They contain Tulipanin, which is an anthocyanin, responsible for allergies, and it induces a dermatitis that affects tulip bulb sorters and florists who cut the stems and leaves. Toxic to horses, cats and dogs, they may cause death.

Cultivation began in Persia, in the 10th century. Not mentioned by any writer from antiquity, so it seems probable that tulips were introduced with the advance of the Seljuks. 1594 is considered the date in the Netherlands. The gift of a red or yellow tulip was a declaration of love, the flower's black center - a heart burned by passion. During the Ottoman Empire, the tulip was a symbol of abundance and indulgence. Today, Tulip festivals are held around the world. Source: Wikipedia.

This poem is a Decuian.

The Decuian (pronounced deck-won), created by Shelley A. Cephas, is a short poem of 10 lines. There are 10 syllables per line and the poem is written in iambic pentameter. The first 5 lines carry the same rhyme scheme of: ababb. But the last 5 lines carry several choices.

So the choices are:

ababbcbcaa, ababbcbcbb, ababbabccc, or ababbcbccc.

For a longer Decuian poem, add more stanzas.

I used feminine iambic pentameter on L 8 and 10.

This photograph was taken by the author himself on May 8, 2016.

CHAPTER 8: SCENES

"What are Scenes?" you might ask.

For the purposes of this book, scenes are poems based on a photograph that says something. It can be an event, or an image that moves you in some way. The purpose of the poem is for the poet to convey the meaning or feeling that speaks to him. Hopefully, it connects with the reader too in that way.

Poem #37

BROKEN BASE
(A Lisalet)

Assemble all the gears that turn.
Rebuild the broken base anew.
The time has come to live and learn.
Deliverance is overdue.

Rebuild the broken base anew.
While dreams ignite and fires burn
find any missing nut or screw.
Assemble all the gears that turn.

The time has come to live and learn.
Forget they said, "You never do".
The future now is your concern.
Rebuild the broken base anew.

Deliverance is overdue,
that hangs here now to twist and churn.
So, chose this chance to carry through.
The time has come to live and learn.

This collection of watch sprockets was on display at a restaurant in downtown Duluth atop the Sheraton Hotel, where I stayed for a meeting of the Capture Minnesota photographer's group. I thought it was interesting. It inspired my thoughts here. Of course, the base can be interpreted in several ways. I thought it fit well for a New Year's Day Poem, when I wrote it.

This poem is a Lisalet.

Lisalet Poem: a style created by Lisa Sherman on FanStory, that has a fixed format of repeating lines and, when rhymed, a forced set of only two rhyme choices in an abab rhyme scheme. The format repeats the first four lines in a structured reverse cascade down the stanzas follows:

1/2/3/4 - 2/5/6/1 - 3/7/8/2 - 4/9/10/3,

such that the stanzas incorporate the repeating lines as

1/2 - 2/1 - 3/2 - 4/3 as the first and last lines of each stanza. Note that while the lines repeat, the meanings transition to new or deeper detail.

The optional rhyme scheme becomes

A1,B1,A2,B2 - B1,a,b,A1 - A2,b,a,B2 - B2,a,b,A2.

The capitals represent the repeated lines. I hope that all makes sense. I chose the syllable count to be 8, but that is not a requirement.

Alliteration: assemble all, broken base, live learn, hangs here, close chance carry.

Caesura: line 10, 15.

Colloquialism: live and learn

Dialogue: "You never do."

Exhortation: assemble, rebuild, chose

Hyperbole: deliverance is overdue, future now is your concern.

Kinesthesia: twist and turn.

Metaphor: dreams ignite, fires burn, hangs here

This photograph was taken by the author in March, 2012.

Poem #38

DIVERSITY
(An Acrostic Poem)

Diversity creates a blend,
Inspired beauty, end-to-end,
Viewed with a non-judgmental eye
Enticing looks, as passersby
Realize that true beauty lies
Shared with a varied bloom bouquet.
It's better with a vast array
That shows uniqueness of them all,
Yet joins them nicely overall.

The world is a more beautiful place when uniqueness is blended. It works for people as well as flowers and plants. We are all a wonderful part of God's garden.

This poem is an Acrostic.

An acrostic is a poem which spells out a word or idea. Usually, what it spells out is the title of the poem itself.

The first letter of each line spells out a key word, or phrase. But variations can be attempted such as having the first letter in the sentence and the last letter in the sentence spell out a word. There is no requirement for meter or rhyme. Although I do believe that they greatly enhance the finished product. Bolding and color coding are also often employed. I added rhyme and iambic tetrameter to this one.

The rhyme scheme is: aabbbccdd.

Alliteration: end to end, bloom bouquet.

Colloquialism: end-to-end.

Caesura: 2, 4.

Enjambment: 3-4, 4-5, 5-6, 7-8.

Hyperbole: inspired beauty.

In-line Rhyme: realize lies.

Poetic imagery: a blend, true beauty, varied bloom bouquet, vast array.

This photograph was taken by the author himself at the Lake Harriet Rose Garden in Minneapolis, Minnesota on August 19, 2013.

EXQUISITE ELEMENTS

(Cinquains and Couplets)

I do hope you'll grant my pardon,
I'll describe a Japan garden.

The breakdown is quite intense,
It has so many elements.

But I will do the best I can,
So you might duplicate the plan.

Garden
Tranquility
Japanese purity
Exquisite element display
Well done

The path
A way to peace
Emotional release
Trail around nature's masterpiece
Calm hath

Pond stones
Of Mother Earth
Adds heavy weight and girth
Quiet dignity yields their worth
Backbones

Water
Is so serene
Providing placid scene
Helps keep the setting clean and green
Savor

A bridge
To walk across
Order from all chaos
Creates a setting of ethos
Image

Trim tree
Branches stately

Adds to garden greatly
Lofty limbs are rather courtly
Beauty

Lantern
Stone human touch
Artistic mood, as such
Mankind's keynote, but not too much
Fat urn

Lotus
Bright blue blossom
Flower truly awesome
An Egyptian sacred emblem
Breathless

In these primary elements
You'll find the seeds of elegance

The Creator's works joined with man's
Quintessential Japanese plans

These are the elements of the Japanese garden. It tried to bring out their essence. They blend natural beauty with human artistic effort to create setting of serenity.

This poem contains rhyming couplets (two lines with rhyming end rhymes) and Cinquains. A Cinquain is uses a pattern. "Cinq." The traditional Cinquain, as developed by Adelaide Crapsey, has five lines and strict structure based on syllable count.

Line 1: Two syllables Line 2: Four syllables

Line 3: Six syllables Line 4: Eight syllables

Line 5: Two syllables

There's no required rhyme scheme, but this poem used one. The rhyme scheme is: abbba in each Cinquain.

Took this photograph at Japanese Garden located at Como Park in St. Paul, Minnesota during September 2013.

Poem #40

FREE WILL
(A Quinquerne Poem)

The paths we take may lead us high or low.
It only takes a moment as we choose.
Our needs and our desires provide the cues
that carry us to many avenues,
and often we're assisted as we go.

The level where we stand may be the wrong one.
The paths we take may lead us high or low.
If we're uncertain, there's a map to show
the choices that prevail at each plateau.
So we may finish journeys, once begun.

There may be steps that help to elevate us,
convenient and so very apropos.
The paths we take may lead us high or low.
It helps us, as we travel to and fro,
to find those steps. They really are a plus.

It's true, regardless whether only shopping,
or learning things in life we ought to know,
those steps that move us may seem rather slow,
the paths we take may lead us high or low,
but choices keep on coming without stopping.

There's always ways to tweak the traffic flow.
The maps and steps will help along the way.
Efficient escalators may convey
us, but we still make choices every day.
The paths we take may lead us high or low.

This escalator is located in the Mall of America in Bloomington, Minnesota. I leave it up to the readers to decide what the steps and maps really are.

This poem is a Quinquerne.

The Quinquerne is a creation of Fanstorian, Pantygynt. It uses ten syllables per line of iambic pentameter. The Quinquerne, as its name suggests, works in multiples of five - five Quintrains of enveloping rhyme (two around three), with the first line, repeated as a refrain line cascading line by line through each Quintrain. The rhyme scheme which, unlike the Quaterne, is essential with this form. The rhyme scheme is

Abbba, cAaac, daAad, eaaAe, afffA, where the capital letter indicates the repeated line.

Feminine endings may be employed, but would not, however, be stipulated as a requirement of the form.

Alliteration: lead low, our our, and are as, where we wrong, prevail plateau, travel to, to those they, choices coming, there's to tweak the traffic, efficient escalators.

Caesura: line 10, 14, 15, 16, 24.

Enjambment: line 3-4, 8-9, 23-24.

Metaphor: paths, escalators, levels, maps, steps, journey, ways, traffic flow.

Kinesthesia: carry us, assisted, travel to and fro, find those steps, keep on coming, ways to tweak, may convey.

This photograph was taken by the author himself in July of 2012.

Poem #41

NATURE'S BEAUTIFUL BOUQUET
(A Rondel Poem)

When the hillsides bloom with color
In Nature's beautiful bouquet,
It's a glorious Autumn day
Where your senses are set astir.

As the skies are turning azure,
Spot this magnificent display
When the hillsides bloom with color
In Nature's beautiful bouquet

In each panoramic acre,
With Autumn leaves all bright and gay,
Lovers can hardly look away.
There's so many sights to savor,
When the hillsides bloom with color..

When out driving around Duluth, Mn. last fall, I came upon this scene.

This poem is a Rondel.

A Rondel is a verse form originating in French lyrical poetry. It is a variation of the Rondeau consisting of two quatrains followed by a quintet (13 lines total) or a sestet (14 lines total). The first two lines of the first stanza are refrains (A and B), repeating as the last two lines of the second stanza and the third stanza. (Alternately, only the first line is repeated at the end of the final stanza). For instance, as A and B are the refrains, a Rondel will have a rhyme scheme of:

ABba abAB abbaA (in the 13 line format) , or

ABba abAB abbaAB (in the 14 line option).

The meter is open, but typically has eight syllables.

Alliteration: beautiful bouquet, senses set, as are azure, autumn all and.

Metaphor: beautiful bouquet

Hyperbole: glorious autumn day, magnificent display.

Kinesthesia: hillsides bloom, set astir, skies turning, turn away, savor sights.

Personification: senses set astir

Poetic Imagery: hillsides bloom with color, skies turning azure, panoramic acre, leaves bright and gay.

This photograph was taken by the author himself along the skyline drive in Duluth, Minnesota, in October 2012.

Poem #42

SUMMER STORM
(A Whitney Poem)

Thunder rolls
In evening sky,
Drenching rains,
Nature clashes,
Light flashes,
Frightening souls
While wet wonder passes by.

Thirsty fields
Drink in their fill.
Rain waters
Make rivers swell.
Once again
Great plenty yields,
The cycle of renewal.

Storms can be frightening, but they are necessary. This storm rolled in to our campground early one morning. This is what I woke up to. After the storm passed, it became a beautiful, bright, sunny day.

This poem is a set of two Whitneys.

The Whitney poem format was created by Betty Ann Whitney. It is a seven-line versed poem based on Japanese patterns with a fixed syllable format that of:

3, 4, 3, 4, 3, 4, 7, syllables respectively.

No rhyme scheme is required, but may be incorporated if desired.

For this poem, I did chose to add some rhyme. The rhyme scheme is:

abcddab abcdead.

Alliteration: while wet wonder.

Kinesthesia: rolls, drenching, clashes, flashes, wonder passes by, drink, rivers swell.

In-line Rhyme: cycle renewal.

Onomatopoeia: Thunder rolls, clashes.

Personification: thirsty fields drink, frightening souls,

Poetic Imagery: drenching rains, nature clashes, lightning flashes, great plenty, cycle of renewal.

This photograph is of a developing summer storm on Lake Superior, taken by the author in September, 2011.

Poem #43

THE CROWD WAS WOW'D
(A Pantoum Sonnet)

He lofted injured raptor to the air.
A flash of furtive feather flaps ensued,
As freedom was released from deep despair
The crowd was wow'd as broken health renewed.

A flash of furtive feather flaps ensued,
Those gathered gasped as nurtured bird arose,
The crowd was wow'd as broken health renewed,
Anticipating paths this eagle chose.

Those gathered gasped as nurtured bird arose.
When sudden burst of energy let loose.
Anticipating paths this eagle chose,
They picked their spot the best they could deduce.

As freedom was released from deep despair
He lofted injured raptor to the air.

I attended a Raptor release. The Raptor Center of Minnesota takes in injured birds, heals them, and releases them again, once they have recovered. They do releases about twice a year. This release was held along the St. Croix River bluffs near Hastings, Minnesota. A very large group gathered along the hillside where it took place. As you can imagine, there were lots of media and photographers in the crowd. Everyone jockeyed to find the best spot to observe, and hoped the bird would fly over them. As you can see, they weren't disappointed.

This poem is a Pantoum Sonnet.

A Pantoum Sonnet combines the characteristics of the two formats. A Pantoum is a repeating poem who's second and fourth lines become the first and third lines of the next stanza. The Sonnet is a 14 line poem with 12 lines of abab rhyming quatrains and a closing couplet. The rhyme scheme for this Pantoum Sonnet is:

A1/B1/A2/B2- B1/C1/B2/C2- C1/D1/C2/D2- A2/A1.

Alliteration: flash furtive feather flaps, deep despair, gathered gasped, was wow'd, let loose.

In-line Rhyme: crowd wow'd, nurtured bird.

Kinesthesia: lofted, furtive feather flaps, arose, sudden burst of energy, picked their spot.

Metaphor: freedom was released, broken health renewed, furtive feathers,

Poetic Imagery: injured raptor, flash of furtive feathers, gasped, anticipating paths

This photograph was taken by the author on September 27, 2014 with his Sony Alpha camera on high speed setting.

Poem #44

THE LOVE BUS
(Rhyming Couplets)

On Selby street in old St. Paul
Just past the quaint Cathedral Mall,

I spotted buses in the rush.
One gave my heart a gentle push.

Displayed, a thought for All of Us,
The message, Love, on big Love Bus.

Above it showed our Heaven's view,
The place to let your soul renew.

With church or bus, there's Love for All!
I found it here, in old St. Paul.

I took this photograph of the Cathedral down on Selby Street, and didn't really notice the sign on the Bus until I loaded it into my computer.

Then I said WOW!

Later, on the site, I saw a prompt to write a Senryu that I thought would work well with this photograph. But got so much critical feedback on all the rules related to that type of poetry, that the original thought got modified again and again, to fit those rules. Although I submitted it to the contest, I felt like I lost the essence I had originally started with, and ended up: dissatisfied, got no votes in the contest, and felt like I wasted this great shot. So this is a new poem, more to my liking and without all those strictures.

This poem is done in Rhyming Couplets.

Rhyming couplets consist of two lines of poetry with end-line words that rhyme. The rhyme scheme of this poem simply is:

aa bb cc dd aa.

Alliteration: On old, Selby Street, big bus.

Caesura: lines 5, 6, 9, 10.

Capitalization for pause and effect.

Folksy Language: in old Str. Paul

Metaphor: Love Bus, Heaven's view. A place to let our soul renew.

Personification: gave my heart a gentle push.

This photograph is the reason that this poem exists, it moved my Muse to express what I saw in verse.

Poem #45

SEARCHED THE STONES
(An Octogram)

On rocky shore of largest lake
They searched the stones,
A treasure hunt where two partake
To probe unknowns.
Amongst the scattered weathered rocks
Gems hidden under Nature's blocks
Are shared, the finds that each one owns.
They searched the stones.

Oblivious of thick'ning fog
They searched the stones.
Unmindful of the hours they log,
That hope condones.
For they are sharing precious time
That each considers most sublime,
Regardless of their tired bones.
They searched the stones.

Took this photograph of my daughter and son-in-law on the shore of Lake Superior one foggy day. This poem seemed to capture the moment of their rock hunting experience. They loved to sit there and look for agates and other pretty stones for hours.

This poem is an Octogram.

The Octogram is a style of poetry invented by Fanstorian Sally Yocom (S.Yocom). It consists of two stanzas of eight lines each, with a very specific syllable count and rhyme scheme.

Syllable count is:

84848884, repeat on second stanza.

Rhyme scheme:

ABabccbB ababddbB, where B repeats same text.

No more than 16 lines.

The tempo is tetrameter on the 8 count line, and Dimeter on the 4 count line, iambic.

Alliteration: largest lake, searched stones, treasure two, one owns, oblivious of.

Elision: thick'ning.

Kinesthesia: searched for stones, probe unknowns, shared, oblivious.

Metaphor: treasure hunt, gems hidden under Nature's blocks.

Hyperbole: probe unknowns, precious time, most sublime.

Personification: hope condones.

Poetic Imagery: rocky shore, two partake, scattered weathered rocks, thickening fog, unmindful of the hours, tired bones.

The picture was taken by the author himself in September of 2011.

Poem #46

WATER'S GIFT
(A Rondeau)

Thou gift of life, whence waters flow,
'Tis evident when flora grows,
Providing picture perfect scenes.
Thy blended hues of reds and greens
Doth touch all life where e'er it goes.

Perchance thy evidence here shows
What any earthbound scholar knows.
Thy precious substance 'tis the means,
Thou gift of life.

Pray that the spark thy touch bestows
Remains as long as starlight glows
Within our seas and deep ravines,
Lest tragic outcome intervenes.
Vitality your drops enclose,
Thou gift of life!

Life exists in the Universe only where there is water, as far as we know. It is such a gift we have on our blue planet, as seen from space. Let's not take it for granted.

I guess this image had me waxing a bit Elizabethan.

This poem is a Rondeau. I was reminded of it this morning as I reviewed an excellent one from tfawcus, a fellow FanStorian, in his Rondeau, The Scream. So I just had to write one myself.

A Rondeau is a fixed form of poetry. It is often used in light or witty poems. It often has fifteen octo - or decasyllabic lines with three stanzas. It usually only has two rhymes (a & b) used in the poem. A word or words from the first part of the first line are used as a refrain ending the second and third stanzas. The rhyme scheme, then, is;

aabba aabR aabbaR.

The format can carry any type of meter or syllable count, as long as it follows the fixed pattern.

Alliteration: whence waters, providing picture perfect, 'tis the, that the thy touch.

Elision: 'tis, e'er.

In-line Rhyme: where e'er.

Kinesthesia: waters flow, flora grows, doth touch, touch bestows.

Hyperbole; tragic outcome, precious substance.

Folksy Language: 'tis, thy, thee, thou, doth, perchance, whence, e'er, pray, bestows, lest.

Metaphor: Gift of life, precious substance, the spark thy touch, vitality.

Simile: as long starlight glows

This photograph was taken by the author himself at the Minnesota Arboretum's waterfall in October, 2014.

CHAPTER 9: SUNRISE/SUNSETS

· ·

This is an area that would own the heart of any poet or photographer. What is more moving than a lovely sunrise or colorful sunset? The beauty and emotions that these release have been the topic of many a bard through the centuries. Many a sonnet has been penned by poets under the spell of these celestial events. Artists and photographers alike revel at the opportunity to capture one.

Poem #47

FIRE IN THE SKY
(An Octogram)

See it! Right at the horizon,
Fire in the sky!
Glowing feast to lay your eyes on,
It'll make you sigh.
Oh, to witness twilight turning,
Getting mixed emotions churning,
While the last daylight is burning.
Fire in the sky!

When the day has finally ended,
Fire in the Sky!
Sun sets scarlet scene, so splendid,
No rules apply.
May inspire poetic fellow,
Or make raging spirit mellow,
To behold the reds and yellow.
Fire in the sky!

This sunset photograph occurred when my wife and I went to Lake Phalen in St. Paul, Minnesota, specifically to watch sunsets. We weren't disappointed.

This poem is an Octogram. The Octogram, a form created by Fanstorian Sally Yocom, is a 16 line poem divided into 2 octets.

The rhyme scheme is:

aBabccbB ababddbB.

The capital letters indicate that line 2 is repeated in lines 8 and 16.

The syllable count is:

8/4/8/4/8/8/8/4 in both stanzas.

I did most of this one in Trochaic meter.

Alliteration: twilight turning, sun sets scarlet scene so splendid, make mellow.

Caesura: Line 1, 5, 11.

Colloquialism: When the day has ended, no rules apply,

Exhortation: see it,

Hyperbole: Oh, to witness, so splendid, raging spirit

Metaphor: fire in the sky

Kinesthesia: glowing, witness, churning, burning, inspire

Poetic Imagery: glowing feast, twilight turning, emotions churning, scarlet scene, inspire poetic fellow, make raging spirit mellow, behold the reds and yellow.

Personification: it'll make you sigh, may inspire a poet.

This picture was taken by the author on the evening of May 19, 2013.

Poem #48

MORNING
(Palindrome Poem)

*

*Morning
Day, Glorious
Sun Bright, Shining
Singing Birds Song
Fresh Air
Rejoice*

*A new Start, We
Today
We Start Anew*

*Rejoice
Air Fresh
Song Birds Singing
Shining Bright Sun
Glorious Day
Morning*

*

This is my second Attempt at Palindrome Poem. Not my favorite format, but I included it here because of my prize winning image.

A palindrome is a word (or sentence) that reads the same backwards as forward. So, the word "Madam" is a palindrome.

For a palindrome poem you incorporate it into your poem but do so with the sentences.

This Photograph was taken by me on a morning in August 2012.

It was taken at Shetek State Park in Southwestern Minnesota.

The birds are Skylarks.

Poem #49

SUNSET ON THE BAY
(Quintrains)

It doesn't matter where you are,
Or if you traveled near or far.
The wonder's never out of reach
At a sunset Beach
With a falling Star.

For sunsets paint a colored sky,
To please the eye of you and I,
In hues that seem to amplify.
As quiet minutes pass,
Forget the hourglass.

To be immersed in blazing bliss,
As tinges touch the sky like this —
A skyline shared, an evening kiss.
We watched it slip away.
Fit end to such a day.

Another sunset on Lake Bronson State Park beach complete with a falling star. I took another Photograph of the same sunset after the sun was completely down and the sky had turned pink and wrote a different poem for it. I wrote this poem for this sky and called the other one The Creator's colors.

This poem is written in Quintrains.

A Quintrain is a five line poem of any rhyme, or meter.

For this one, the rhyme scheme is:

aabba, for each stanza.

The syllable count is:

8,8,8,6,6.

Alliteration: blazing bliss, tinges touch, skyline shared, we watched.

Caesura: line 13

Colloquialism: It doesn't matter where you are, near or far, forget the hourglass, fit end

Kinesthesia: traveled near or far, falling star, tinges touch, we watched, slip away

Hyperbole: wonders, please the eye, hues amplify, blazing bliss

In-line Rhyme: where are, eye I,

Metaphor: wonders out of reach, hourglass

Poetic Imagery; sunset beach, falling star, colored sky, tinges touch the sky, such a day

Personification: sunsets paint

This photograph is the reason that this poem exists, it moved my Muse to express what I saw in verse. The photograph was taken by the author himself in September, 2012.

Poem #50

SUNSHINE FINALLY PIERCES
(Quatrains in Coupled Rhyme)

Sunshine finally pierces through utter gloom,
As it trickles through the windows of my room.
Morning daylight gives the pleasure I derive
From the fascinating fact that I'm alive.

Another day that I cherish wispy breeze,
Or the Cardinals singing softly in the trees.
The setting sun painting colors in the sky
Another day to savor, before I die.

To appreciate a closeness with my wife,
Who has shared with me the ups and downs of life.
Once again bedeviled by beguiling charms,
Kissed and cuddled, as I wrap her in my arms.

When I feel the sun's warm rays upon my face,
Watching birds soar with such stunning style and grace,
While the waves are splashing hard upon the shore,
Don't I wish life could go on forevermore?

But, the last days will sadly come , for us all,
Hoping when it does, I'll hear the angel's call.
Then, sunshine will no longer pierce through the gloom
As it trickles through the windows of my room.

Emotions have overcome us all at one time or another. It could be from someone that broke our heart or just life in general. This is just a Poem about having another day.

This poem is written in Quatrains.

A Quatrain is a poem of four lines with any rhyme or meter. This one is done in odd numbered syllable count of 11. This was to accommodate an anapestic meter. I'd classify this as mixed meter, as it varies.

Alliteration: trickles through, daylight derive, from fascinating fact, singing softly, setting sun sky, with wife, bedeviled by beguiling, feel face, watching with, soar such stunning style, while waves, splashing shore.

Caesura: line 12, 17, 18.

Hyperbole: utter gloom, fascinating fact, cherish, stunning, splashing hard, go on forevermore

Irony: another day to savor, before I die, but the last days will come.

Kinesthesia: pierces, trickles through, wispy breeze, kissed and cuddled, wrap her, watching birds, waves are splashing

Metaphor: Ups and downs of life

Onomatopoeia: Cardinals singing,

Personification: sunshine pierces, sun painting,

Poetic Imagery: sunshine pierces the gloom, singing softly in the trees, day to savor, bedeviled by beguiling charms, feel the sun's rays, watching birds soar, stunning style and grace, hear the angel's call.

Question: Don't I wish life could go on forevermore?

Photograph is the Author's. It was taken on the North Shore of Lake Superior in September of 2011.

GLOSSARY OF POETRY TYPES

www.ingramcontent.com/pod-product-compliance
Lightning Source LLC
Chambersburg PA
CBHW080959120626
46546CB00010B/2967